Junior High Book One
The Elements of Art and Composition

Written by Brenda Ellis
Developed by Brenda Ellis and Daniel D. Ellis
Edited by Ariel DeWitt and Daniel D. Ellis
Cover and Book Design, Creative Cory, Technique, and Project pages illustrated by Brenda Ellis
Works after master artists on Vocabulary pages by Naomi C. Bapple
Illustrations and photos on pages 14, 38, and 41 by Daniel D. Ellis
Student artists are acknowledged beside their works as they appear in the text.

Second Edition

ACKNOWLEDGMENTS

Many thanks to my husband, Daniel Ellis, for his part in developing this curriculum and for taking care of a multitude of other tasks to make sure this project was completed. Thanks to Christine Ann Feorino for her suggestions and editing of the first edition. Thanks to Naomi Bapple for her fine illustrations. Thanks to all the families who participated in testing the curriculum. Thanks to all the students who participated in the lessons and to those who let us share their work with others through this book. Thanks to Dover Publications Inc., NY and Art Resources, NY for supplying the fine art images by the great masters.

Copyright © 1999, 2005, 2007, 2008 by Brenda Ellis

All rights reserved. No portion of this book may be reproduced – mechanically, electronically or by any other means, including photocopying – without written permission of the publisher. Please don't compromise the educational value of this book by photocopying images. Students cannot see what a pencil drawing should look like when tonal values are reduced to black and white.

Printed in the U.S.A.
ISBN 978-0-9815982-6-0

Published by
Artistic Pursuits Inc.
Northglenn, Colorado
www.artisticpursuits.com
alltheanswers@artisticpursuits.com

THE Curriculum for Creativity!™

ARTistic Pursuits®

JUNIOR HIGH BOOK ONE
THE ELEMENTS OF ART
AND COMPOSITION

Brenda Ellis

A COMPREHENSIVE
ART PROGRAM
DESIGNED TO
INVOLVE THE
STUDENT IN THE
CREATIVE PROCESS
WHILE DEVELOPING
OBSERVATIONAL
SKILLS

Art Instruction
PLUS Master Works Featuring World Art

Property of: HACIL Charter School
To Return: Call 715-934-2112

Getting Started

CONTENTS

Page	Unit	
2		Contents/ Art Supplies
3		What Parents Want to Know
4		What Students Want to Know
5		**The Elements of Art**
6	1	Space
11	2	Line
16	3	Texture
21	4	Shape
26	5	Form
31	6	Value
36	7	Line in 3 dimensions
41		**Composition**
42	8	Visual Paths in Line
7	9	Center of Interest
52	10	Balance, Symmetry
57	11	Balance, Asymmetry
62	12	Rhythm
67	13	Space Without Depth
72	14	Space With Depth
77	15	Perspective
82	16	Proportion
88		Evaluation Sheet
89		Bibliography

ART SUPPLIES

First Semester:
- 2 each – drawing pencils HB, 4B
- 1 – vinyl eraser
- 1 – metal pencil sharpener
- 1 – sandpaper block
- 1 – sketch pad for drawing
- 1 – wire (aluminum or light weight types)

Second Semester:
- 1 – pen or marker pad
- 1 – waterproof drawing ink, black
- 1 – brush, round #8
- 2 – pen nibs, #101 Imperial or similar nib
- 1 – pen holder

Additional Items: drawing board, wire cutter or pliers, modeling clay

DRAWING BOARD: A drawing board can be purchased at art supply stores, or can be cut from a small piece of 3/8 inch hardboard, found in lumber yards. Cut it to 15" x 16" for a small board, or 18" x 18" for a large board. The drawing board gives you a consistently smooth surface to draw on and is portable so you can draw anywhere. Use two large binder clips to hold the paper onto the board.

Getting Started

What Parents Want to Know
Book Content and Scheduling

To learn to draw artists have always focused on two groups of topics known as the elements of art and principles of design (composition). Each unit in this book introduces one of these topics over four lessons. Each topic is explored in unique ways, giving students enough experience with the topic that they naturally incorporate it into the way that they draw. It becomes part of their thinking as they draw any kind of subject matter. This kind of focus, paired with ample opportunity to practice is how children learn to draw.

First Lesson of Each Unit

Building a Visual Vocabulary
Here students are given a topic to focus on explained in words and pictures. The creative exploration assignment guides students to observe the topic in their own environment. They make connections to real-world experiences and create a work of art from their observations and ideas. The assignment for this lesson is colored gold.

Second Lesson of Each Unit

Art Appreciation and Art History
Students see how the topic is used in a work of art by the masters and apply their new observations to a work of art that they create. Students gain knowledge of artists and art history.
The assignment for this lesson is colored gold.

Third Lesson of Each Unit

Techniques
Students learn how to use the materials and tools while applying that knowledge to make an original work of art. The assignment for this lesson is colored gold.

Fourth Lesson of Each Unit

Application
Students do a final project incorporating the new techniques and topic while using a variety of references such as still life objects, landscapes, portraiture, photographs and more!
The assignment for this lesson is colored gold.

Scheduling Art Class

CLASSES PER WEEK: TWO   TIME PER CLASS: ABOUT ONE HOUR
PERIOD: 32 WEEKS OR FULL SCHOOL YEAR

This schedule can be modified to fit yours. Keep in mind that students can work independently so it is their time you are scheduling, not your own. Schedule art class at a time when they can complete the art assignment, even if it runs over an hour. Once interrupted, students can rarely return to an activity with as much enthusiasm as they first had. Time for completing each activity will vary greatly depending on students' approaches, however, you should see that as they learn to use more of the elements within their pictures that they are taking more time on each piece.

Getting Started

What Students Want to Know
The Mysterious Language of Art

If the secrets of great artists were contained in a book, would you open it? We hope your answer is YES! There is much to learn from artists who have created all their lives. The first great secret artists share with others is:

> ## 1. Learn to observe the world around you- to really see it.

"OK", you say, "I'm looking and I see the same things I've always seen." We won't let you get stuck there. The second part of this secret is:

> ## 2. Learn *what* to look for.

We tend to look at subject matter and make vague and arbitrary decisions about what we see. Comments such as "grass is green," "faces are hard to draw," and "I can draw a horse from the side, but not from the front" all show that we are focusing on the subject and not on what we see. If you've ever made statements similar to these you are simply focusing on the wrong type of information. As you look at the world in the ways artists do, and this book is designed to show you just what those ways are, your art will greatly improve.

So do artists really *see* differently? After all, we all have the same kind of eyes and unless impaired in some way, we see the same as everyone else. Artists have learned to focus on a particular aspect of what they see and at the same time block out other types of information. The language of art includes code words called the elements of art. You may have heard about these elements which include space, line, shape, texture, form, value, and color. The next secret of artists tells us how to see the world using these elements.

> ## 3. Learn to *focus* on one element of art at a time, while drawing, and *block out* the others.

With practice your mind can focus on any element of art you choose. Your mind can switch with lightning speed between elements, making it a powerful focusing and blocking out tool.

The Elements of Art
Ready, Set, Go!

Now that you know why you should learn to focus on the elements of art such as space, line, shape, form, and value, it will benefit you to take a certain type of approach when drawing. We will call this the Ready, Set, Go approach.

READY YOUR MIND!
Just as athletes must adopt a mindset that pushes them beyond what they have accomplished in the past, artists must have a mindset that allows them to achieve greater things. They strive to get closer to their goals in each drawing. Just as the athlete stumbles occasionally, the artist will experience a few failures as he attempts to try new things. Accept that this will happen and that it is a necessary part of improving your skills. Understand that there is more than one way to accomplish any single artistic task. Creativity comes into play, as the artist finds new ways of seeing, new ways of drawing, and an accomplishment that is truly personal. Doing your own thing is encouraged. True art is not about copying a technique. True art is not about being as good as someone else. True art is about exploring your own strengths in the arts as you use the lessons in each unit to bring new information, to inspire, and to generate ideas.

SET UP YOUR MATERIALS!
Nothing turns off the inspiration to draw quicker than not having the materials available when you need them. The moment when inspiration comes is the moment to put it on paper. By the time a missing tool is found the inspiration to draw has left. Keep all drawing materials together in one spot, including all paper, so that you have what is needed when it is needed.

GO FOR IT WITH ENTHUSIASM!
One must have a goal in mind in order to stay enthused about a particular subject. In the past your own goals may have spurred you on to improve your artistic skills. Those same goals will work for you as you go through this book. Begin to use those elements and techniques introduced in each unit in your drawings. Ready your mind! Set up your materials! Go for it with enthusiasm!

A Quick Sketch and a Finished Drawing
You will make two types of drawings. One is called a sketch, or study. It is a quick drawing that has you focusing on one specific topic while you draw. These types of drawings take about 10 to 30 minutes depending on what you are asked to do and really help with your ability to see as an artist sees. Other drawings are more finished. In a finished drawing, you will use all the knowledge you've gained up to that point and put it on paper. These can take as long as you need, possibly and hour or more. Just be aware of the two types of drawings so that when asked to make two or three sketches in one assignment, you understand that you are developing skills that you can use in the finished drawings.

Lesson 1

UNIT 1
space

Vocabulary and Creative Exercise

Space is the area of the paper that you draw into. The white cat and cushion are centered within the space of the page. They also fill the space. The space around the cat is made dark in this drawing after a painting by an unknown American Folk artist. The original painting is titled, *Tinkle, a Cat*. Begin to see your paper as a space that is to be filled as you draw.

Be Creative

You CAN draw! Drawing is a matter of coordinating the hand with what your eyes see. With practice it becomes as easy as writing your name. For handwriting we train our hand to make small strokes that fit neatly on lined paper. For art we train our hand to make larger strokes that fill up the whole sheet of paper. Take on the following drawing challenge. Write your signature in the upper right hand corner of a white sheet of paper. Since you've done this on school papers for years you'll find it very easy. Write your name again, this time stretching it across the page so that it begins on the left edge and ends on the right edge. The letters have to be written large enough to reach. If you did not succeed try again until you do.

Congratulations! You've successfully used the skills it takes to draw a picture. You looked at an object (your written name), evaluated its shape, made visual judgements about space, and made large enough strokes to fill the page. You drew a picture of your name and it only took a short time to get it right.

OBJECTIVE: to understand that artistic ability is not a talent possessed by only a few gifted people, but a skill that any individual can learn.

CREATIVE CORY

Cory always takes the assignments a little further than the rest of us, doesn't he?

6

Lesson 2

Look at Space in Art

Art Appreciation

Portrait of the Elephant, Dal Badal, Chasing His Attendant. Artist Unknown. Mewar Period in Rajasthan, India. 1750
Photo Credit: The Pierpont Morgan Library/ Art Resource, NY

Dal Badal, the star of this scene, takes up 4/5 of the space of the page. The remaining 1/5 is left for his attendant on the run. The horizontal space fits the long shape of the elephant. Positioning him to the left allows room for the elephant to seemingly move through the picture, toward the attendant.

Paper turned to the **Horizontal** Position

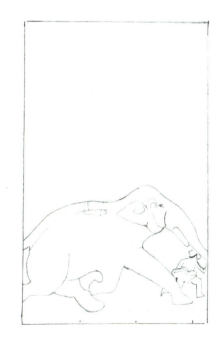

Paper turned to the **Vertical** Position

Dal Badal's story is not told nearly as well in the vertical position. It leaves too much empty space at the top and not enough space at the bottom to show the action clearly.

7

The Cultures
EAST AND WEST

Since the 19th century there has been an exchange of ideas in the arts between the Eastern cultures of Asia and the Western cultures of Europe and America. Even today there is a strong interest in Japanese art called "Anime" among young Westerners. To distinguish various artistic influences within our world we talk about cultures. A culture is not restricted to the boundaries of a country. Culture is a set of social behaviors. It affects the art people make, their beliefs, and the traits of a group of people. Cultures change. These changes can occur when a culture conquers another by force or influences another through contact. Today we divide cultures into certain categories to communicate their differences more clearly. We call the painting of Asia "Oriental" and it includes the art of India, China and surrounding countries, plus Islamic art of the Middle East. Western art refers to the art that developed in Europe and the territories they spread to, including North America. The terms East and West will be used throughout this book to describe these large cultural groups.

The Art
PAINTING IN INDIA

Indian art has primarily been created for religious purposes. It is difficult for Westerners to enter into the strange world of fierce red gods and demons displaying symbols of their power. These types of images dominate Eastern religion. Westerners relate better to Indian miniature painting, which developed from the 16th to 19th centuries. It began with a Mughal Emperor, Akbar, who studied art as a child. Once establishing himself as Emperor of India, he invited Persian and Hindu artists to record his great deeds. Their works show complex landscapes with Akbar as a hunter and warrior. Akbar hoped to unite the religions of Muslim, Hindu, and Christianity and so he had many examples of European goods at court. His son and grandson continued the artistic and educational traditions established by Akbar which emphasized learning both Eastern and Western ideas. Schools of art were established in India and Mughal art was a guiding influence for centuries. The scene on the previous page was part of a painted album. Like our photo albums of today it was designed to feature portraits, but these were portraits of royal elephants. Whether humorous or frightening, this portrait of the elephant, Dal Badal tells a clear message about Dal Badal's power, size, and temperament as he chases his attendant. Indian miniature paintings tell the stories of their characters with clarity and simplicity.

Art History

The Challenge

The beauty of Indian miniature paintings is in the clear shapes of the figures. Make a simple drawing of the painting on the previous page on a 9x12 inch sheet of paper. Make a second study on a half sheet. Draw freehand by observing, do not trace, omit details, and draw the edges of the elephant and figures so that they fill up the space on each paper size. Small studies like this will help you to place lines within the space of the paper. You are developing skills in observation.

HOW TO MAKE A ROUGH SKETCH   Lesson 3

A rough sketch is a drawing that is put down quickly on paper. With a rough sketch, the artist can try out different ways of placing the object within the space of the paper before doing a more lengthy drawing.

Understanding Your Pencils
Drawing pencils are numbered according to the hardness or softness of the graphite. The HB pencil marks the middle of the range. H pencils have hard leads. The larger the number is on the H pencils, the harder the lead is. Hard pencils make light lines. B pencils have soft leads. The larger the number is on B pencils, the softer the lead is. Soft pencils make dark lines.

Starting the Sketch
A general rule is to start a sketch with light lines and finish with darker lines. Decide how much of the scene you want to show in the drawing. Place the paper horizontally if the object is long. If the object is tall, place the paper vertically.

Draw lightly, with the HB pencil. Make corrections by drawing over the first lines. Erasing is not necessary in a rough sketch. A rough sketch may have many lines as corrections are made as shown in the middle example. Include what is around the vehicle, showing trees, road, and fence as shown in the final example.

Try New Techniques

Make a rough sketch of a favorite subject. When you draw, look at the object you are drawing. Concentrate on placing the subject within the space of the page. Omit details. It may take some practice to make the marks big enough.

The Project

Lesson 4

Application

Read the story below. After reading the story of *The Blind Men and the Elephant*, draw an illustration of it. As you draw, consider the placement of objects within the space of the page.

One day six blind men came upon a friendly elephant. The first blind man stretched his hands in front of him and felt the elephant's flat, rough side. "This elephant is like a high, strong wall," he announced.

The second man, who was standing near the elephant's head, put his hand on its long, sharp tusk. "Not a wall. I would say that it's more like a spear."

The third man put his arms around the elephant's leg. "I hate to contradict you," he said, "but I believe that the elephant must be like a tree."

The fourth man reached high and touched the elephant's ear. "All of you are wrong," he said. "The elephant is comparable to a fan."

The fifth man was standing by the elephant's back end. He grabbed the animal's tail. "I don't understand the confusion," he said. "I'm sure I am correct in saying that the elephant is like a rope."

Now the elephant was a bit playful, and ornery, so he tickled the sixth man with his trunk. The frightened man stepped back and said with a shiver, "Remain calm everyone, but I know that the elephant is really a huge snake!"

"No way!" "Never!" "You are quite wrong!" "Absolutely not!" argued the others. They went on their way, disagreeing, and never bothered to put their heads together to understand what the elephant was really like.

Student Gallery

To learn, you must be more curious about the world than these six blind men were. You must not be satisfied with seeing one part of a thing. Wouldn't the blind men have known more if they had taken the time to put all the pieces together? This book will help you put the pieces together so you have a good understanding of the subject of art. We challenge you to use the ideas you are presented with in each unit. Put your best efforts into the drawings and we think you'll be excited with your progress.

Student Work: by Nathaniel Ellis

Materials

HB drawing pencil
4B drawing pencil
Vinyl eraser
Pencil sharpener
Drawing paper

References

Use imagination and references from the following sources:
- Refer to a real elephant at a zoo
- Find a picture from the encyclopedia or a book
- Find a picture on the web

LOOK BACK! Explain the placement within your picture. Did you focus on the elephant, placing him in the center of the picture or did you place the characters on the page in a different way?

Lesson 1

Vocabulary and Creative Exercise

Lines are drawn within the space to create an image. Lines can vary from light to dark when using pencils. The image of the girl jumping rope is drawn with line. This image is taken from part of an ink drawing by Ben Shahn, called *Girl Jumping Rope*. Wonderful works can be made with a simple drawing tool, paper, and line.

Be Creative

Pick subjects that appeal to you when you draw. Use your interests as a guide to good subject matter. Science studies on birds, planes, habitats, or the body can lead to drawings of those things. Hobbies or sports make good subject matter for drawing because you are already familiar with the objects or people you depict. History lessons and Bible stories offer great material for drawing people in action. Often our interests are in those things that are around us. Begin to look at your surroundings for subjects to draw.

Go outdoors, if possible, and look for an object from nature that has something unique or interesting about it. Make a drawing of it. It can be a quick sketch. Spend at least 15 minutes on the drawing.

OBJECTIVE: to think about personal preference when choosing subject matter for drawing and to expand one's ideas of acceptable subjects for drawing.

It is a perfect example of an object from nature, Lyle. It's interesting, impressive, and real!

Lesson 2

Look at Line in Art

Art Appreciation

Utagawa Kunisada, 1786-1865; *A Horse under a Willow*, 1830's
Photo Credit: Dover Publications Inc.

Japanese line has an expressive quality because of the way the line moves, curves, and goes from thick to thin. In this ink painting we see the Japanese fondness for graceful curves. To draw a horse with as few lines as possible and with lines that so clearly describe the curved shape is a highly valued skill in Japan and China. The large shapes of the mane and tail would have been accomplished using a large brush and, like the line across the horse's back, made with a single stroke. Although a pencil does not lend itself to as much variation in line as a brush, you can see how line variation plays an important role in art.

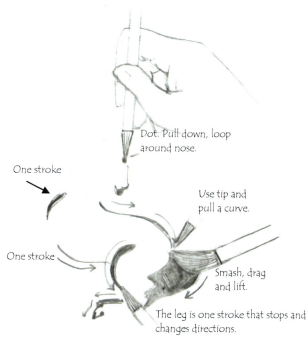

One stroke

Dot. Pull down, loop around nose.

Use tip and pull a curve.

One stroke

Smash, drag and lift.

The leg is one stroke that stops and changes directions.

The Culture
JAPAN INSPIRED BY CHINA

Imagine meeting someone so wonderful, that you wanted to copy everything they did. Perhaps you have a younger sibling that looks up to you in that way. That is how the Japanese felt about the Chinese people they met in 500 A.D. when they came into contact with mainland China. They believed that Chinese culture was superior to their own and adopted the Chinese writing system of calligraphy and their artistic traditions. The writing system was composed of unique groupings of expressive line. The Chinese used black ink that produced different tones depending on the amount of water mixed with ink. Their brushes made many kinds of lines. Strokes with brush and ink went from thick to thin. They curved and dotted with quick precise movement. This line quality is the predominate element used in Chinese art. Graceful and elaborate, these strokes were practiced and refined for centuries.

The Artist
Utagawa Kunisada (1786 - 1865)
JAPANESE WOODBLOCK PRINTMAKER

Kunisada made many woodblock prints in his lifetime, some paintings, and book illustrations. Woodblock prints were designed by the artist, and then reproduced by others for sale in the 19th century. Americans and Europeans were enthusiastic purchasers of Japanese woodblock prints. Kunisada's most famous designs are kabuki actor portraits. Kabuki is the traditional form of Japanese theatre and is known for its elaborate costumes and make-up. The art shows actors in costume and displays the props used on stage. Kunisada was so prolific that it is estimated he may have produced between 20,000 and 25,000 designs for woodblock prints during his lifetime!

Art History

The Challenge

Make a rough sketch of the painting by Kunisada. By doing so, you will practice using your pencil in curved motions to develop a form. Use lines similar to those seen in the work. We work from other artist's works to better understand what they did, not to make an exact copy. Do not try to be perfect, just observe! Next, find photographs of horses in other positions. Draw them on the same sheet of paper, using the curved lines as you did in the first drawing.

Chinese horse designs.
Photo Credit: Dover Publications Inc.

HOW TO USE GRAPHITE PENCILS

Lesson 3

Techniques

THIN AND THICK LINES

To make thin lines, sharpen the pencil with a sharpener often and rotate the pencil in your hand occasionally as your draw. To make thick lines rub the pencil lead against the sandpaper block, making the tip flat. Use the sandpaper block often to keep the flat shape.

Thin, sharp marks are great for showing edges and making crisp lines!

Drawing Using Sharp, Pointed Pencils

Thick, broad marks are great for filling in space!

Try New Techniques

Sharpen one HB and 4B pencil to a fine point. Shape the other HB and 4B pencil to a broad tip using a sandpaper block. Make two drawings, one with the sharp pencils and the other with the broad tip pencils. Compare the results of the two drawings.

Drawing Using Broad Tipped, Flat Pencils

The Project

Lesson 4 — Application

Don't worry about mistakes as you draw. No one gets it perfect the first time. One method artists use so that they can correct mistakes easily is to draw the first lines lightly, using the HB pencil. The lines can be drawn over until you are pleased with the placement. There is little use for erasing. Once things are placed correctly on the page the artist begins to use a darker mark with the 4B pencil. Try this method. Make a drawing from a photograph that uses thin and thick lines with an HB and 4B pencil.

Student Gallery

Student drawing of an eagle: by Michael Saragosa. Notice the light lines that were drawn first. Heavy lines were drawn over the light ones for the finished work.

Materials

HB drawing pencils
4B drawing pencils
Vinyl eraser
Pencil sharpener
Sandpaper block
Drawing paper

References

Draw an object found in a photograph. Photographs can be found in the following places:
- Photo album
- Nature magazines
- Encyclopedia set
- Non fiction library books

LOOK BACK! Did you begin by drawing light lines, freely changing them until you were pleased with the placement? Did you use thick and thin lines in the final drawing?

Lesson 1

UNIT 3
texture

Vocabulary and Creative Exercise

Texture is the look of the surface of an object. It can be imitated using different types of marks or lines. Long, curved lines describe the texture of this porcupine drawn after a woodcut by artist, Leonard Baskin titled, *Porcupine*.

Be Creative

Experience! Artists through the centuries have practiced creative exercises to help them see. Even Leonardo da Vinci, who is known for his mathematically precise approach to art, told his students to look at clouds and rocks to see pictures in them. You may have tried seeing things in the clouds. Did you know that by doing so you were practicing creativity?

Choose one object and ask, "How many ways can this thing be experienced?" The object may be a tree. If so, touch the bark, feeling its texture. Climb high in its branches, staying to contemplate the view. Lay beneath it, looking up into its branches. Hug it. Then draw your insights or a new view that you had of the object. Look at the object often to gather details as you draw.

OBJECTIVE: to discover new views when looking at an object, create some unfamiliarity, in order to practice better observation skills and a need to look at the object more closely.

CREATIVE CORY

I appreciate creativity Cory, but don't you think five days under a tree is a bit much?

Lesson 2

Look at Texture in Art

Art Appreciation

In this work of art we see four distinct types of marks made by the artist. These marks do not show us outlines, but instead describe the textures of the objects. You can use a pencil in different ways to show texture.

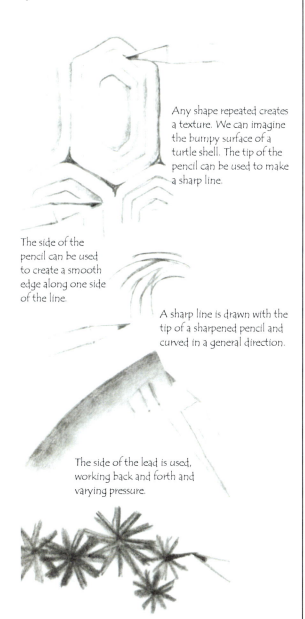

Any shape repeated creates a texture. We can imagine the bumpy surface of a turtle shell. The tip of the pencil can be used to make a sharp line.

The side of the pencil can be used to create a smooth edge along one side of the line.

A sharp line is drawn with the tip of a sharpened pencil and curved in a general direction.

The side of the lead is used, working back and forth and varying pressure.

Lines radiate from a center point outward to create shapes. When these shapes are repeated texture is created.

Hokusai, *Swimming Turtles*, 1832-33
Photo Credit: Dover Publications Inc.

The Culture
THE EAST DEVELOPS CONTEMPLATIVE ART

While Western cultures developed a taste for realism that dominated the look of their art, Eastern art was not bound by how "real" the object appeared. This allowed them to focus on a more emotional response to the things they saw. In *Swimming Turtles*, Hokusai has focused on the feel of water, and the feel of turtles floating and gliding through it. We even get a beautiful sense of the way underwater plants move with the motion of water. Although the turtles look very realistic, the water does not. It shows the "idea" of water. Eastern culture was much more aware of the human experience using all human senses, emotions, and feelings about what is seen. The practice of meditating on objects within nature and the high value they held for the natural world affected their art. While contemplating water for hours the artist could be inspired by some aspect of it. They would then show that quality about water. In contrast the West developed a strict set of rules for accuracy in what they saw. We will discuss the reasons for those rules in later lessons. For now, keep in mind that East and West developed different ideas about art according to the values the societies thought were important. Art is always a reflection of values.

The Art
TRADITION OF COPYING

Have you ever used or seen "How to Draw" books? These books give exact methods for how to draw specific types of subjects in specific positions. This is how the Oriental artist learned to paint. Methods were developed for how to draw a rock, a tree, or a mountain. Students copied the masters' strokes. They did not look at real nature until they had perfected the methods of portraying the specific things they would see there (343 Lee). In this way there was a model that would be carried out for centuries by all artists that followed it. Because of this, it is difficult for the non-expert to distinguish one artist from another. The artist who carefully used the specific techniques of tradition was highly regarded in the society. He was not thought of as just a laborer, but as a trained and gifted master. Eastern art had little need for originality which is so highly praised in the West.

The Challenge

Create an underwater scene. Use some of the textures that are shown on the previous page. You may enjoy creating water in the way Hokusai shows us. Do so by first drawing the sweeping lines with the tip of the pencil. Place the other objects into the picture. Do not use the side of your pencil for completing the water yet. This technique lays a lot of graphite onto the paper which will smear easily. Think about plants that grow underwater and invent specific strokes to show the texture of those plants. Add animals or fish to your scene. Once the animals, fish, and plants are finished, complete the water.

Remember to draw subjects that you enjoy as you explore new ideas. You can get pictures of water creatures from the internet, encyclopedias, or books.

HOW TO DRAW TEXTURE

Lesson 3
Techniques

Textures can be imitated by careful observation of the real thing and making marks that describe the texture. You can also draw texture by transferring it to the paper through rubbing. Both techniques start by showing the curves of the creature through simple lines. Then marks are added inside the lines.

The mark making technique has two steps. The artist creates an outline of a rabbit. Then repeated parallel marks are made with a pencil that has a flat tip to create the texture of fur. Close observation of a real object is helpful when drawing the texture.

Examples of texture through mark making are shown in the blocks below.

Examples of texture through rubbing are shown in these samples.

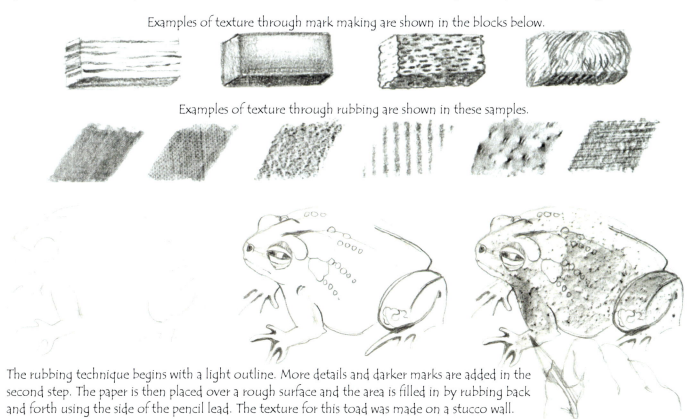

The rubbing technique begins with a light outline. More details and darker marks are added in the second step. The paper is then placed over a rough surface and the area is filled in by rubbing back and forth using the side of the pencil lead. The texture for this toad was made on a stucco wall.

Try New Techniques

Draw two separate pictures of objects, one showing marks to make texture, and the other a sample of rubbing.

The Project

Lesson 4 — Application

Draw a picture that shows a variety of textures. Use different kinds of marks to describe the kinds of textures in each area of the picture. In this drawing you may use both drawing and rubbing methods within the same picture.

Student Gallery

Materials

HB drawing pencils
4B drawing pencils
Vinyl eraser
Pencil sharpener
Sandpaper block
Drawing paper

References

Look for textures in photographs of your favorite objects. When drawing textures from a photograph, make sure the object is close enough that the texture is clearly seen.

Student Work Above: by Phillip Bradrick. Notice the different kinds of marks Phillip uses to show the texture of the bear.

Student Work at Left: by Adam Gutierrez. Adam uses a wonderful mark to show the texture of the grass.

LOOK BACK! Did you look for a photograph that clearly showed texture? Did you use different kinds of lines or marks to draw texture?

Lesson 1

UNIT 4
shape

Vocabulary and Creative Exercise

Shape is defined by the outside edge of something: its outline. This drawing, which is after a Crow artwork titled, *Tipi liner with Battle Pictures*, uses flat shapes, outlining the horse and rider. Traditional Native American drawings deal with shape as the main element.

Be Creative

A student went to a major city and was fascinated by the height and closeness of the buildings. He immediately made sketches of his observations. Reflecting on the experience one day, he was inspired and set about constructing his own skyscraper designed from wire. The final project required thought and more creative energy than the original sketches. By sketching the inspiring sight he had experienced it in a deeper way and was then able to create.

TIME TO EXPERIENCE! A meaningful experience happens when we allow ourselves time to look, feel, and be a part of something. TIME TO THINK! With time, one can process those experiences and create from them.

Find a building or other piece of construction that you've not paid attention to in the past. It may be something you've never seen before in your travels, or a familiar site. Make a sketch of it. Look for shapes, patterns, and sizes. Think about the purpose of the structure. How is it designed to fit the needs of the people who use it? What changes could be made to improve it?

OBJECTIVE: to see a common object in a new way and to encourage further development of ideas and subject matter.

CREATIVE CORY

"Dear Lyle and Janet, Finally found the right building…just drew my one-thousandth stone. Your friend, Cory"

Lesson 2

Look at Shape in Art

Art Appreciation

Katsushika Hokusai (1760-1849); *Beneath the Wave off Kanagawa*, 1830-32
Photo Credit: Dover Publications Inc.

Water has a unique ability to become any shape. Here the artist uses little finger shapes for the surf to demonstrate the peril of the fishermen in boats. The heads of the men are a repeated shape that gets our attention. The shapes within this painting are all curved. There are no sharp angles or box shapes. Curves create a rhythmical quality to the work. And as we know from tides and wind on water, it flows in a rhythmical pattern.

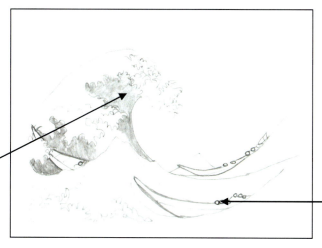

Dark values help define or emphasize the shapes of the waves.

The boats nearly disappear. The round shapes of the men's heads help them stand out.

22

The Culture

VISUAL EXPRESSION

Shape is a primary element seen in all Japanese art. While shape is the clearest way to show the immediate appearance of an object, we cannot assume that shape is only used to describe what the object looks like. Japanese artists use shape to describe a "feeling". "The shapes become a form of personal expression which cannot be portrayed through the literal copying of surface appearances (Okvirk 45)." In Japan, where copying the master's strokes and way of doing things was so strictly adhered to, the style of an artist appeared in the way they envisioned shapes within the picture space. As seen in *Beneath the Wave off Kanagawa*, by Hokusai (1760-1849), the water is transformed in the artist's mind into a type of monster with greedy hands. It reaches out to consume the men and their boats. Giving inanimate objects human characteristics is called personification and is often used in literature. To describe this picture we might say the watery fingers threatened to tip the boats. We know that water does not have fingers, but it creates a powerful visual image. Here Hokusai personifies by use of visual means.

The Artist

Katsushika Hokusai, (1760-1849)
JAPANESE UKIYO-E PAINTER

This painting, also called *The Great Wave*, by Hokusai, is one of the most famous Japanese prints known in Western society. Surprisingly, it does not follow traditional Japanese style, nor is landscape painting a traditional subject matter for the Japanese prints. The Japanese consumer preferred samurai and actors portraits. Hokusai was a bit of a rebel. He liked to play with new ideas. This very non-traditional full landscape includes common fishermen, who were looked down upon in their society. The idea of landscape painting came to Japan from the West. The works of Dutch painters, who had made landscape painting popular from 1600- 1700's in Holland, were produced as cheap illustrations. Dutch merchants smuggled goods into Japan, wrapped in artists etchings, used as throw-away wrappers. Hokusai and other artists learned about perspective through these discarded works and transformed Dutch landscape painting into something that was Japanese. Later, as these Japanese prints were so well received and created in large numbers, they were discarded and used as packing material for imports going from Japan to Europe. The Impressionists, working in the late 1800's would be greatly influenced by the work of Hokusai. They picked up his simplicity of form and pattern. And so European art was mixed into Japanese art and then sent back to Europe where it would return the favor.

The Challenge

Look carefully at the way shape is used in the painting on the previous page. Shapes are exaggerated to create a feel of water. Think of an experience with moving water that you have had. You may have a fountain at home or a running faucet that you can observe. You may put something in the sink that the water can run over or into. Observe the motion for a time. Then on paper, exaggerate the motion you see and create a drawing of that motion using shapes to define the water.

HOW TO MAKE INTERESTING SHAPES

Lesson 3

Techniques

It is important to choose subjects and themes for your art that have personal interest to you. You must also remember to choose interesting shapes. See your subjects as shapes. Once you set up a group of objects, test them in the following three ways to make sure they have visual interest:

1. Look for contrasts such as tall and short, big and small, curved and irregular. Check this by beginning a line on the left side of the paper. Draw around the tops of the objects, making a silhouette of the group. The example on the right has many contrasts: smooth curves, irregular shapes, straight lines and different heights.

2. Avoid too much empty space such as sky, background, floor, surface, wall, etc. See the empty space better by shading in all areas that are not objects. The empty space (shaded area) in the drawing on the left has variety and interest. In the drawing on the right there is too much empty space because objects are placed too close to the bottom of the page and are too small. The objects are all the same height and are spaced evenly apart with no overlap, adding little visual interest.

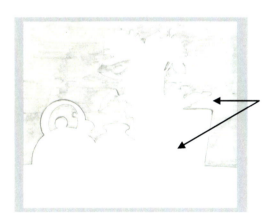

This drawing shows a good balance of empty space and positive space.

This drawing shows too much empty space.

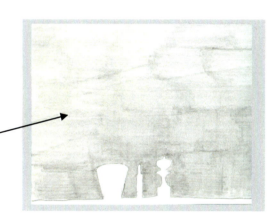

3. Finally, check light and dark shapes. Instead of drawing objects with outlines, shade in the dark shapes. Turn everything into a black and white pattern. The leaves and tea kettle handle intrude into the white space. The white reflection on the tabletop (under the framed photo) and the space between the pot and kettle intrude into the dark space. An interesting pattern of shapes appears.

Try New Techniques

Arrange a group of objects. Check the shapes for interest by making one of the three types of sketches shown on this page. Adjust the arrangement if needed. Recheck, and finish the work.

The Project

Lesson 4
Application

Draw a picture of an animal from a photograph. Look for the shape of the animal as well as other shapes in the picture. Include the area in front of and behind the animal.

Student Gallery

Photographs from calendars are large enough to see well.
Photographer unknown.

Materials

HB drawing pencils
4B drawing pencils
Vinyl eraser
Pencil sharpener
Sandpaper block
Drawing paper

Student Work: Unknown. In this work, the student was able to capture the feel of the wolf. They also drew shapes that feel like the packed snow in the photograph. They used dark lines in the wolf face, and lighter lines for snow.

References

Find a picture of an animal from a photograph. Make sure the animal is clearly seen in the photograph before you begin working from it.

LOOK BACK! Did you look for shapes in the picture and try to draw them? Did any of the shapes in the picture overlap?

Lesson 1

UNIT 5
form

Form is the roundness or thickness of the object. There are many ways to make an object appear to have form. One way is to show a light and a dark side like we see on an object when light shines from one side. Another way is to draw lines that follow the curve of the object. We see both ways used in this illustration of a work by Honore Daumier titled *Poor France! The Trunk is Blasted...*

Be Creative

Place your hand on a piece of paper and draw around it. You probably haven't done that in a few years. Compare the drawing of the hand to your actual hand. How would you describe the drawing? Think about it for a moment. Would you use the words, "shape", or "flat" to describe the drawing? How would you describe your hand in relationship to the drawing? Look at thickness, light and dark areas, texture and details.

Place the hand you do not use for drawing on the table in an interesting way. Pose in a way that bends the fingers, and is not just flat with fingers spread out. Draw a picture of your hands including some of the things you just described it as having. How will you show the roundness of the fingers and the thickness of the palm?

OBJECTIVE: to draw the hand in a way that only shows shape and to explore ideas for showing the hand as a form with thickness, roundness in two drawings.

CREATIVE CORY

Cory's finished and I'm still trying to get the first line right. What's he know that I don't?

"Don't erase mistakes or you will always be beginning at the beginning. Keep right on drawing over first lines."

Lesson 2

Look at Form in Art

Art Appreciation

Vincent van Gogh (1853 – 1890); *Man Reading the Bible*; 1882
Photo Credit: Dover Publications Inc.

Form can be shown in line. In this drawing Van Gogh uses lines in different directions to show the form of the man and his clothing.

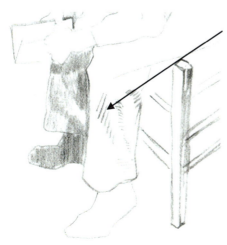

These lines follow the folds in the pant leg.

These lines wrap around the torso, following the form of the body.

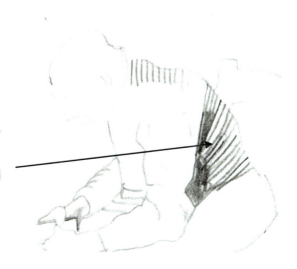

27

Art History

The Culture

THE PURSUIT OF REALISM IN THE WEST

As Europe slowly exited the dark ages, people became consumed by the idea of a new classical age. They wanted art to reflect the grandeur which the ancient Greek and Roman Empires had displayed. The beginnings of this new classical age took place in Italy, what had been the heart of the Roman Empire, but it quickly spread throughout all of Europe during the 14th – 17th centuries. This Renaissance "rebirth" brought new discoveries of perspective and proportion and set in motion a pursuit of concrete reality in painting and sculpture. Reality, making paintings that looked as much like the real object as possible, became the only accepted means of making art within Europe. This idea began to turn around in the 19th century. New ideas in the structure of society, including the disastrous French Revolution, which led to dictators like Napoleon, gradually changed people's minds about traditional governments and traditional art too. Toward the end of the 1800's the Impressionist artists attempted to show a reality that changed quickly, just like their governments had changed. Japanese prints, which made their way to Europe at that time, showed a simplified form of reality which appealed to the Impressionists. Some showed the effects of light in a particular moment and the effect of color in a moment in time. This early work by Van Gogh still reflects the traditional values of creating a realistic figure and using proportion that was so well perfected in 16th century Renaissance Period. However, it also shows a departure from absolute reality in the way Van Gogh makes the marks. Dark and heavy, the lines are left for us to see. It is not smoothly blended as any Renaissance artist would have completed it. The move away from absolute reality happened within the lifetimes of the Impressionists.

The Artist

Vincent van Gogh
(1853 – 1890)
DUTCH POST IMPRESSIONIST PAINTER

Vincent van Gogh is one of the most famous painters in modern times. His earliest works were of the people he served while he was a pastor. He felt compassion for their impoverished state and poor living conditions. He drew and painted many portraits of the families, men, and children. Here he shows a man reading a Bible. While his first works focused on people, he later painted landscapes. He'd become depressed about his inability to help people, largely due to a hot temperament that he wasn't able to change. He began to look at color and landscape painting as a way of showing his morals. He believed that the colors within nature could show us the attributes of God. In this way he painted "ideas" like the Japanese, and not the solid reality of Renaissance Europe.

The Challenge

Draw a sketch of the drawing by Vincent van Gogh for the purpose of studying how he used lines to show form. Use the soft lead of a 4B pencil to draw dark lines. You may want to use a broad point to make wide lines.

HOW TO DEVELOP OBSERVATION SKILLS THROUGH CONTOUR DRAWING

Lesson 3 — Techniques

CONTOUR

The contour drawing is a type of quick sketch in which you keep your eye on the object as you draw edges. To make a contour drawing start on one side of the object and draw the outside edge, or contour, of the object as you look directly at it. The key is to keep your eyes on the object most of the time and move your hand to follow the movements your eyes make. Eye and hand move at the same time. As your eyes follow the edge of the object, your hand records its shape on paper.

To the left the artist draws her own hand holding a very large pinecone. The drawing isn't perfect, but that is not the point of contour drawings. As we draw in this way, we train our hand to follow what we see with our eyes. The more we train, the better we see and draw!

CROSS CONTOUR

Another type of contour drawing, called cross contour drawing, helps you be more aware of the internal form of an object. Here you look at the object and draw lines across the form that describe the direction of the form and the roundness of the form. Start at the top and without lifting the pencil, work across the form to the bottom. In the drawing above the artist lifts the pencil from the page only a few times.

Try New Techniques

Choose objects that have interesting contours such as an egg carton or branch with leaves. Make a contour drawing focusing on the outside edge only. Then try the second method, making a cross contour drawing.

The Project

Lesson 4
Application

There are many types of contour drawings that artists practice. One type that you may want to try is called the blind contour. In these drawings you do not look at the paper at anytime during the process. You keep your eyes only on the outside edges of the object, drawing the line at the same time your eye travels around the object.

For this project expand what you can do with a cross contour drawing. Here you will explore the interior form of an object. The student drawing below shows lots of line variety. The artist did this with a pointed pencil, laying it on its side when he needed more width. One continuous line goes from thin to thick.

Student Gallery

Student work is by Dan Ellis. Circ. 1974.

Materials

HB drawing pencils
4B drawing pencils
Vinyl eraser
Pencil sharpener
Sandpaper block
Drawing paper

References

Position yourself to work from direct observation as you look at the object. Interesting objects are all around you. You could look for the following:
- Shoes
- Potted plants
- A pile of clothing

LOOK BACK! Did you work from direct observation? Did you keep your eyes on the object most of the time as you drew the inner form of the object? Does your drawing show variation in the line?

30

Lesson 1

UNIT 6
value

Vocabulary and Creative Exercise

Value refers to the lightness or darkness of the object when compared to other objects or to the value scale. The sides of these peaks are of different values, depending on how much light they receive. Values range from white to black, with many grays in between. This scene was drawn after a work by Umetaro Azechi called, *Remains of a Volcano*.

THE VALUE SCALE

light   middle gray   dark

Be Creative

Suppose you are given a grapefruit, a lollypop, and an apple. You are told to arrange them by degrees of sweetness going from sweet to sour. You would most likely begin with the lollypop, placing the apple next to it, then the grapefruit. Just as you can successfully arranged by degrees of sweetness you can arrange things by degrees of light.

Gather 10 small objects that are gray, tan, black, or white. Arrange these objects by degrees of lightness from the lightest object to the darkest object. With pencils, draw areas of gray which closely match each of the objects. The result will be patches of gray on the paper which most closely represent the value of each object. Do not draw a picture of the object, only its value. This can work no matter what color the objects are. Colors have light and dark values too.

OBJECTIVE: to observe value in everyday objects and to make visual judgements as to the value of those objects.

CREATIVE CORY

THE OUTER LIMITS OF THE VALUE SCALE, by Cory

Lesson 2

Look at Value in Art

Every object has local value that describes how light or dark it is. A red apple has a darker value than a yellow apple. The green in a cucumber is darker than the green in celery. Learning to see values correctly is one of the most important skills you will need as an artist. The human eye perceives or understands objects by their value differences.

Diego Rivera, *Elisa Saldivar de Gutierrez Roldan*, 1946.
Photo Credit : Dover Publications Inc.

When light shines onto an object the values change. It becomes lighter in the direction of the light and darker where no light hits it. You can see this change in the dark green curtain and on the green stool that the woman sits on.

Our mind wants to focus on "things" such as the skirt, the legs, or the stool. When we do this we see parts as separate from the whole picture and our value judgments can be off without our even noticing. To practice seeing the picture as a whole, begin to make quick sketches like this one, breaking the picture down into only three values: light, medium, and dark. Your drawings and color work will have more strength when you begin to focus on values. Can you see by this quick sketch how the artist has used values to emphasize this woman? The darkest value surrounds her creating the most intense contrast to her light skin and clothing.

32

Art History

The Culture

MEXICO; LAND OF TURMOIL

Mexico's indigenous people were quite different from each other. Some cultures were peaceful and others were extremely violent and feared. European explorations changed these cultures from 1500-1800 when Spain claimed the land of Mexico, including the area we now know as the Western part of the United States. The Spaniards ruled and governed Mexico and forced some natives to work for them. In 1810 Mexicans gained freedom from Spanish rule, but new Mexican leaders quickly became dictators and did not help the people of Mexico. They used their power to make themselves rich and kept people in fear by killing ruthlessly. One very poor leader, Santa Anna, caused Mexico to loose half of its territory to the United States in 1847. Revolution and civil war continued in Mexico until the 1930's. Many people living in the United States today are descendants of those who lived in the Mexican territory that the United States acquired. Many have come from Mexico since that time.

The Artist

Diego Rivera (1886 – 1957)
Mexican Mural Painter

In the 1920's Diego Rivera and José Clemente Orozco were famous Mexican mural painters who hoped to encourage the population of Mexico with paintings on large walls in public buildings. They painted the history of Mexico. Rivera painted scenes of Mexico's past with gentlemen and ladies in colorful traditional costumes doing common labors in peaceful times. Orozco painted the violent scenes he witnessed throughout his lifetime. His art is harsh and reflected the Mexico people lived in at the time. Both artists worked in the United States when their situations in Mexico became threatened. In a free country they thought that they could freely paint their political views, often forgetting that the individuals who hired them did not hold the same views. Rivera thought communism was the answer to people's troubles and painted a mural glorifying the communist ethic in contrast to capitalism. While his controversial view caused a stir in national news, people liked his well composed real figures painted in real spaces and in a stylized manner that appealed to the tastes of the time. Many American mural painters, hired by the United States during the depression, were inspired by the work of the two Mexican artists, Rivera and Orozco. They both finished their careers in Mexico and continued to paint murals until their deaths.

The Challenge

Set up a lamp or set an object beside a window so that there is a single light source shining on the object. Place the object near a wall, so that its shadow is cast onto the wall. Draw the object. Include the shadow and shade in the form of the object, This example is by Jared Baughn.

HOW TO SHOW FORM WITH VALUE AND LIGHT

Lesson 3

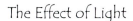

Local value refers to the lightness or darkness of an object without the effect of direct light. The local value of an object does not actually change, however it appears to change when light is present.

Local Value
The local value of each area includes: white clothing, middle value skin, darker value background, and darkest value in the hair.

The Effect of Light
As light shines onto each area the values change. Notice that the value of the shadow on the white cloth is lighter than the value of the shadow in the face.

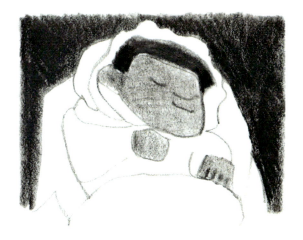

Try New Techniques

Draw an object that has a local value in the middle value range. Look for light and shade. Divide the object into three distinct values: white showing the lightest areas, middle gray showing the local value, and dark showing the shaded areas. An example is shown on the right.

The Project

Lesson 4 — Application

Form is seen on any 3-dimensional surfaces if they receive light. Place an object on a table and direct a light onto it. Light that shines from a single window works well. Make sure that you can see a light side and a darker side on the object. Draw areas of light and dark to show form on the paper. Remember to use your softest pencil (4B) to make very dark marks.

Student Gallery

Student works by Michelle Stegmiller. Both are drawn from wooden figures.

Materials

HB drawing pencils
4B drawing pencils
Vinyl eraser
Pencil sharpener
Sandpaper block
Drawing paper

References

Choose simple objects from around the home. Some objects might be the following:

- A bottle
- A figurine
- A bowl
- A basket
- A lampshade
- An egg
- A ball

LOOK BACK! Did you set up the object so it had one direct source of light? Did you include light and shaded areas in the drawing? Did you build up the shaded areas working from light to dark?

Lesson 1

line in 3-dimensions
UNIT 7

Vocabulary and Creative Exercise

We can think about a wire as a line in 3-dimensions. It can be bent, twisted, wrapped, and changed in many ways to become an object that has real form.

To see some incredible wire sculpture, visit the following web site:
Animal art by Elizabeth Berren at www.wirelady.com.

Be Creative

Curiosity is a key to opening the door to creativity. You will want to open that door because it is creative people who write songs that others sing, draw pictures that others admire, and make new products that other people use. Creative people act because their curiosity pulls them in directions of exploration. There is a thrill in doing something that no one has done in quite the same way. Think about the truly creative people you know. Do they follow the activities and interests of others or do they follow their own interests and curiosities? How can you become a more creative person?
1. Follow your interests. What things most fascinate you about your world? What are you curious about? Find out about those things.
2. Explore your interest through a different type of medium: sculpture.

Bend, twist, and create the form of an object using wire. The form is easiest to handle when made about three to five inches tall. The runner above is 12 inches tall. You can add other materials to your wire sculpture such as fabric, beads, or small accessories that you build.

> OBJECTIVE: to gain experience in sculpting a 3-dimensional form. This unit requires imagination and visualizing a form from all sides.

Lesson 2

South African *Imbenge* basket artist Jaheni Mkhize demonstrates "soft basket" construction in Santa Fe, July 2005. Photo Credit: Indigo Arts Gallery Inc., Philadelphia, PA.

South African Imbenge baskets. Photo Credit: Indigo Arts Gallery Inc. Philadelphia, PA

Art Appreciation

The Object

The visual arts of all cultures most often take two forms: the depiction of an object onto a flat surface and the making of an actual object. One we call painting or drawing and the other we call sculpture. Objects made by indigenous cultures were usually made from whatever natural materials were available such as plant material, stone, clay, or bones. Native North American cultures carved animal and animal-human forms from wood or modeled them from clay. In an area with no trees or clay available, the Inuit, indigenous people of Alaska, Greenland, and Canada, carved small sculptures of animals and human figures from the ivory and bone of the walrus. The Zulu people of South Africa wove grasses into baskets. Objects such as these were often functional as well, and used as boxes, pipes, or baskets. Today, in the West, we often separate functional items as crafts and non-functional as art. Contrary to that idea, the indigenous people of the world tend to make functional items that, when decorated, tell who they are as a people. This is often their means of artistic expression.

The Art

South Africa's Zulu people create tightly woven baskets from grasses and palm leaf. These ***ukhamba*** baskets inspired those living in urban areas to create a new kind of basket, the ***imbenge*** basket. It is woven from a material that is easily available in modern times: recycled telephone wire. The baskets are bright. Today people in craft cooperatives in the neighboring nation of Zimbabwe have developed their own distinct style of telephone wire basket. Telephone wire is thin and covered with colorful plastic. It is good for weaving or wrapping around heavier pieces of wire.

See the next page for your wire construction assignment.

The Challenge

You make a stand-up wire construction following the directions below.

A drawing has two dimensions, length and width. It is flat. In this project use a flat drawing to create a "wire drawing". Then, create a base and stand it upright.

This wire sculpture of a train engine uses additional blue wire and a coil base.

1. Draw a simple outline of the object you've chosen on a piece of paper. This line drawing is the template. At the beginning of your wire, leave eight inches free to use for the base, and then bend the wire as you follow the lines in your drawing. Bend the wire around the template until you come back to the bottom from the other side. Add any additional pieces of wire to the outline. (The tire swing was added at this point in the example.)

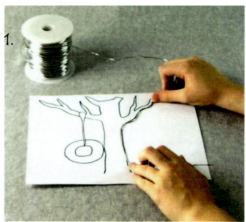

2. At the base, twist the two ends of wire around each other and insert into a base of modeling clay, so that it stands up.

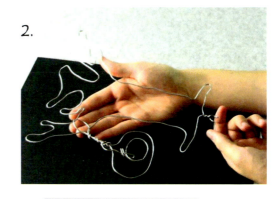

3. Place the modeling clay onto a piece of cardboard of the same size, to protect table surfaces. Display your wire sculpture.

HOW TO MAKE A HANGING MOBILE

Lesson 3
Techniques

Create small sculptures in wire, and then hang them to together to make a mobile. Before you begin, you need a theme. Possible themes are planets, birds, flying insects, famous buildings of the past or ancient warriors with weapons, as shown below. Create something that has interest to you. Choose a wire that is sturdy enough to hold the shape you want to give it. Heavy wire and lightweight gold and copper wires were used in the figures below. Add other items as well. Pieces from costume jewelry already have holes drilled and are easy to incorporate into the mobile design by stringing the wire through the pieces. Once pieces are made, you are ready to hang them.

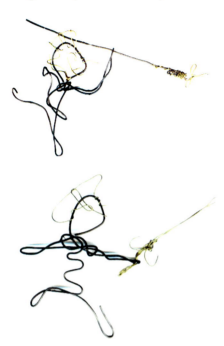

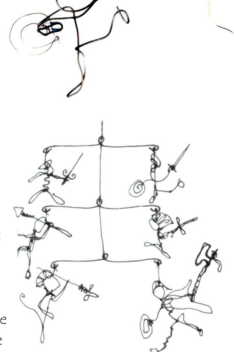

When you have finished the pieces, put the mobile together. You will need string or fishing line, heavy wire, scissors, and pliers. Cut wire with pliers. Cut string with a scissors. Never cut wire with a scissors. It will leave gashes in the blade.

Twelve warrior figures were designed by Nathan Ellis. Once into the project, he found that creating realistic pieces with the heavy wire was difficult, so he made the figures abstract and focused on helmets, weapons, and accessories. Here we show six of the twelve ancient warriors from different cultures.

Bend two or three pieces of heavy wire with pliers, to create beams.
Loop and knot a string into the center of one beam. Hang the beam from a nail in a doorway, hook in the ceiling, or open space, so that it moves freely as you work. Tie a string to two objects you have completed and attach them to the ends of the wire beam. You can adjust the placement of the string by sliding it along the wire beam in order to balance the objects. Objects of heavier weight will need to have the string moved in toward the center of the wire beam. Lighter weight objects can move out toward the end of the wire beam.

Attach a string to the center of the first wire beam and to the center of a second wire beam, connecting the two. Attach two more objects to the second beam in the same way that you attached the first two. Continuing in this way, you can make as many levels as you want.

The Project

Lesson 4

Application

Make a wire sculpture. Use any subject that is of interest to you. Here we show a fish.

1. You can wrap wire around a cardboard template. When finished, slide the wire form off the template. The fish below was started in this way.

2. For the head and tail, make a loop with the wire and twist the ends together. Then bend the loop into the shapes you want. Pinch, twist, and cut wire with a needle nose pliers.

3. Aluminum wire is soft and can be pounded flat for a great effect. Once a shape is formed you can pound the wire flat with a hammer on smooth cement.

4. The body will have two loose ends. Attach the head and tail by wrapping the lose ends around the head or tail. Display your wire sculpture on a stand or hang it.

Wrap the wire's end around the tail shape to secure.

not hammered

hammered

Student Gallery

Student work at the left is by Heather Wilking. She uses aluminum and colored wire. The body was wrapped around a cardboard tube then twisted tighter at the tail.

Materials

- Any type of wire (aluminum wire can be pounded flat)
- Materials for decoration
- Material for a base
- Needle nose pliers
- Hammer (optional)

References

Look for a picture or photograph of the subject you choose to make from wire.

COMPOSITION

A poem by Edgar Guest begins, "The things that haven't been done before, those are the things to try" (Bennett 488). Artists are constantly searching for new ideas and new ways to work with images. One study that will greatly help in producing new and exciting images is the study of composition. Composition is how the artist arranges the elements of art on the page. As you discover new ways to arrange the objects within your pictures, you'll learn to make art like you've never done it before!

Composition is the arrangement of line, shape, texture, form, and value within the space of the page. Those elements can be arranged using:
- Visual Paths
- Center of Interest
- Balance
- Rhythm
- Depth
- Perspective
- Proportion

In this section of the book you work with ink. Ink can be applied with a brush or with a pen. These two methods of applying the ink to paper give very different results, as shown above. We hope you have fun exploring this exciting new medium.

Lesson 1

visual paths
UNIT 8

Vocabulary and Creative Exercise

Creating a visual path is one way to achieve balance. Line can create a path for the eye to follow which leads it through the picture space. The line of the circus ring leads the eye from the horse, around the circle to the rider. The eye then goes from the rider to horse and around again. This drawing is after a work titled *Circus Rider* by Henri de Toulouse-Lautrec.

Be Creative

Just as a good writer rewrites, the artist makes changes in their art. Artists do not immediately see what is in front of them. The lines, movement, or true colors only emerge as the artist studies the subject. The artist cannot draw it perfectly with the first lines any more than a writer puts creative thought, correct grammar, and composition together perfectly in the first draft.

When working in a medium that covers up underlying layers, like oil paint or acrylic paint, this redrawing happens right on the canvas. When working in a medium that cannot be reworked, the artist does the same subject on many sheets of paper, reworking line, shapes and movement until it appears right.

Try redrawing to get a better composition. Choose a group of objects that appeal to you. Arrange them in a row and make a quick sketch of the group. Improve the arrangement by overlapping some items and make a new sketch. If you can think of another way to group the items, do so, then make a final sketch. You may notice that you draw with more accuracy as you make more drawings.

OBJECTIVE: to change the arrangement of the objects and to draw with more accuracy as the objects are studied in different positions.

Lesson 2

Look at Visual Paths in Art

Art Appreciation

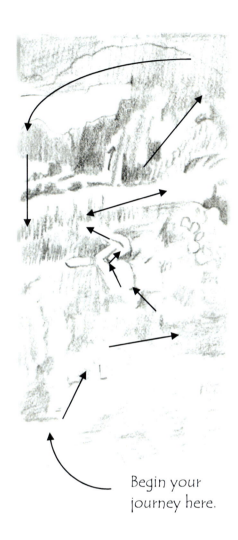

Begin your journey here.

The Chinese hanging scroll is a type of painting not found in Western cultures. The paintings were designed to be viewed on special occasions and one looked at them in a slow contemplative manner. Move your eyes through the painting like you would take an actual hike up the path. Think about the things you would see along the way.

Tao-chi (Shih-t`ao) (1641-1707) The Jingting Mountains and Waterfall in Autumn. 1671. Ink on paper, 86 x 41.7 cm. Photo: D. Arnaudet Photo Credit : Réunion des Musées Nationaux/ Art Resource, NY.

43

The Culture
CHINESE FORMS OF PAINTING

Chinese culture developed three forms of painting. These three, the hand scroll, hanging scroll, and album leaf, had very different dimensions because of their functions. All three forms were made on either silk (cloth) or bamboo (paper).

The hand scroll never developed in Western societies and is purely an Eastern form of art. It is stored rolled up, is horizontal and in extreme cases can be as much as 40 ft. long. As the scroll unrolls it tells a story, like a movie, from beginning to end. Held in both hands the viewer unrolls on one side and rolls on the other, simultaneously to allow a small portion of the scene to appear. They are viewed right to left, opposite of how a Westerner would approach the task. They also include comments about the artwork (written in words) which early viewers wrote directly onto the artwork.

Hanging scrolls were wider, but much shorter. They were stored rolled up and then unrolled for special viewing times. They are usually vertical in format like the artwork we just looked at.

The album painting is much like a picture designed to fit in a book. This format was practiced in both Eastern and Western cultures.

The Art
HOW TO LOOK AT CHINESE ART

Nature painting thrived in China because of Taoist and Confucian belief systems. Trees, rocks, water, and mountains were seen to follow the same natural laws as those established for the heavens and earth. For example, people observed that the form of a pine tree was "noble" and "solitary" and a pine is like the "moral character of virtuous men (343 Lee)."

Art training in the West teaches us to look at the entire picture at once. We focus on the place the artist has emphasized through the use of light or lines. Our eyes travel here or there but are always guided back to the place we started. This approach makes viewing a Chinese work just plain confusing. We might ask what part we are to look at. The Chinese format, either very long or very tall, seems to present too many possibilities at once. But if we think about how the hand scroll was used, we understand that it was not created to be rolled completely out and viewed all at once. We begin at the beginning (the right side) and move slowly to left, as we enjoy the surprises that are presented on our journey. When viewing a hanging scroll begin at the valley, the bottom, and slowly travel upwards on your visual journey until you reach the highest mountain peaks. Stop to rest your eyes on a spot every once in a while, just as you would if you were actually walking along the path.

The Challenge

Organize a work of art that creates a visual path as Chinese painters did. As you draw the objects concentrate more on the areas that reinforce your visual path and do less detailed drawing in the areas that do not enforce the path. You might do this by making darker lines to enforce and lighter lines to attract less attention.

HOW TO USE BRUSH AND INK

Lesson 3

Set up the following items:
- open ink bottle
- a container of water to rinse the brush in
- a paper towel
- paper for ink work
- soft hair watercolor brush that comes to a point when wet

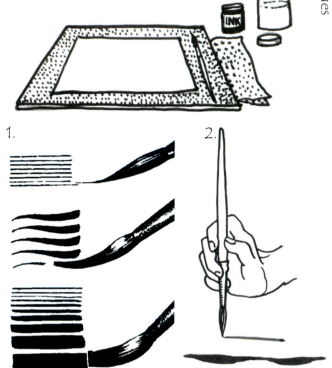

1. Practice using the brush by drawing lines of varying widths. The brush is soft and responds easily to pressure. Vary the pressure to make smooth lines ranging from very thin to very thick.

2. Use the Chinese method of holding the brush in the vertical position. When manipulating the brush, do not only move the fingers but the whole arm. This allows a wider range of movement and control of the line. Rinse the brush thoroughly when finished.

Try New Techniques

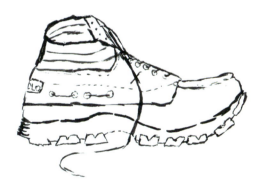

Student work on the right by Carolyn Perea uses heavy lines. Student work on the left by Colby Bowser uses thinner lines of varying widths.

Make lines of various widths while drawing interesting footwear. Set a shoe in front of you and paint contours with a brush.

The Project

Lesson 4 — Application

Choose an object to draw and arrange several objects around it. Remember to create a visual path so that the eye goes from one area to another and back again. Then draw the arrangement in pencil making any corrections needed. Finish with brush and ink. The pencil lines can be erased after the ink has completely dried.

Student Gallery

Student work on the right is by Kelly Boatwright. She made a visual path by centering a light object between two dark objects. The patterns on the light vase make lines that carry the eye from one side to the other. The plants are interesting shapes and bring the eye to the top of the picture. Also the eye is helped to the top because the stripes on the white vase get darker as they go from the bottom to the top.

Student work at the left is by Erin Craven. By overlapping objects that have very different textures we look at all three items going from one to another.

Materials

Pencil
Vinyl eraser
Black ink
#8 watercolor brush
Paper for ink
Water container
Paper towels

References

Use a group of three objects that are different in some way. Work from real life.

LOOK BACK! Did you use marks or value to move the eye around the picture? Point out the path that the eye travels.

Lesson 1

center of interest
UNIT 9

A painting will be more interesting if the focus is in one area. Often a center of interest can be created by using light. Here the center of interest is the stage. Light from the stage is reflected onto the viewers, and then our eye goes back to the brightly lit stage. This drawing is after a work by Honore Daumier titled, *The Drama*.

Be Creative

Fresh ideas for art images are all around but are often missed. Just as it is difficult to isolate and identify a single drop on the skin during a rainstorm, it is difficult to isolate single ideas, inspirations, and visual material for art purposes. A tool is needed to collect these ideas and direct them into something useful. As gutters around a roof collect raindrops, ideas can be collected on many sheets of paper. The artist catches these ideas on paper as fast as they come to mind or to sight. As the gutter directs the downpour into one area, the artist later directs the collection of ideas by tossing the failures and keeping the best work. This gutter approach will work if you keep the following in mind:

1. There are many right solutions and techniques.
2. Everything that comes to mind is WORTH recording. (It can be eliminated later.)
3. An idea or thought should not be judged before it gets on paper.
4. Some of the works will be better than others.

Try this approach by positioning yourself in a place that is somewhat unfamiliar to you like a back porch or room you are not usually in. Draw sections of the place turning your view first to one area then to another. Draw several objects as they are seen together, such as the neighbor's house and car parked in front or a group of trash cans with trees behind them. Create six rough sketches. These should be drawn quickly, about five minutes each. Then examine the drawings and decide which ones are best and why. Do this evaluation after works are completed, not while the drawings are being made.

OBJECTIVE: to become familiar with the process of sketching many works as ideas or scenes that come to mind and to understand that editing work is a process that happens AFTER the work has been created. Many students edit ideas in their minds before they ever try to put them on paper.

Lesson 2

Look at Center of Interest in Art

Art Appreciation

Our eyes are naturally attracted to certain types of things. A light shining in the darkness catches our eye. Our eye will make leaps from one light area to another. By arranging the light areas of a painting, the artist can point the eye in certain directions, creating a center of interest.

Diego Velasquez, *Las Meninas*, c. 1656.
Photo Credit: Dover Publications Inc.

Here we show the light areas as dark so that you can better see the shapes. The shapes lean in toward the center object (the little girl).

48

The Culture

FROM CHURCH PAINTERS TO PAINTERS OF KINGS

Art was made for European cathedrals during the Middle Ages. A cathedral was the central focus of a town and was often built in the center of the town. Artists, called craftsmen, thought about themselves as being part of a community, working together for the spiritual purpose of glorifying God with displays of gold and richly painted surfaces. With the Protestant Reformation in the 1600's, came a call to rid churches of art, both paintings and sculptures. The decline in the need for church art forced artists to look for people outside the church who needed their services. At the same time, leaders of towns became leaders of countries and kings gained more power and control than they had before. New wealth from sea explorations and trade in the New World was pouring into the hands of European kings and noblemen who sponsored the trips and a new focus on individual greatness arose. Kings needed artists to make paintings and objects that would glorify the king. They built palaces as grand as any cathedral. They adorned the palaces with paintings of themselves, along with marble sculptures. Silver and gold from the New World decorated their ceilings. Ornamental dishes and richly detailed furniture were also a part of the grand decorating scheme. Kings and nobles, in an age of incredible wealth, hired artists to supply these goods in order to properly impress others. To supply beautiful paintings was the purpose for art and no one questioned it (Gombrich 361). "Beauty" became the new standard that art would be judged by in the eighteenth and early nineteenth centuries. This was the age of Kings and a good time to be chosen as "First Painter to the King."

The Artist

Diego Velázquez (1599-1660)
Spanish Court Painter

Velázquez was born in 1599 in Seville in southern Spain, an important city with a thriving artistic community. He studied art as a boy with artist, Pacheco. In 1623 Velázquez was asked to paint a portrait of the young King Philip IV. Philip was so delighted with the result that he immediately appointed Velázquez as one of his court painters, and from then on would allow no one else to paint him. The move to the royal court in Madrid gave Velázquez access to the royal collection of Italian paintings, which greatly inspired him. He also was allowed to travel in order to study. He learned the style of Caravaggio, making figures look real and placing them in dark backgrounds. He was highly successful, rising up the ranks in the royal household and became responsible for Philip's public image. His paintings and décor were to make King Philip look good. He was put in charge of the decoration and modernization of the royal residences.

The Challenge

Draw a quick value sketch of an object that is light, using a dark background to create a center of interest. Limit the drawing to no more than four values. Do not be concerned with details as you draw. Concentrate on values.

HOW TO COVER LARGE AREAS

Lesson 3

Techniques

Dip the bristles partly into the ink as shown. Pull the brush across the edge of the jar to remove excess ink.

Fill in large areas of black easily and quickly with the brush. A wide stroke can be made when the brush is dragged across the paper while applying just enough pressure so that the bristles fan out. The brush is held in a slanted position, much like a pencil is held, but do not let your hand rest on the paper.

Make lighter values by using a mixture of water and ink. Place a few drops of water in a lid or small container and add a drop of ink to it. Test the value on a scrap piece of paper before applying it to the artwork. Lighter values are seen in the house pictured below.

Try New Techniques

Use this picture or a photograph as your reference. On a full sheet of paper, paint large areas using the slanting hold. Control the edges, focusing attention on the tip of the brush. Concentrate on values. If you want a sharp edge, allow one area to dry before painting up to it. If you want a soft edge, paint up to a wet area and allow one value to bleed into the other.

Here the light area was wet and the darker value runs into it for a blurred effect, called a soft edge.

Here the light area was dry when the dark area was brushed over it. This produces a sharp edge.

50

The Project

Lesson 4

Application

Plan a drawing that frames a figure or group of objects. The objects may be viewed through a doorway or any type of entrance, gate, etc. Look for value changes that will emphasize the figure or objects. If there is not enough contrast of light and dark, as the artist, you can exaggerate the values. Work in pencil or ink.

Student Gallery

This student work by C.J. features three trees, framed by a doorway. Their shadows and dark branches create interest. They are also emphasized by the contrast in values to the hill in the background.

This is a student work by Dan Ellis (cir.1975). The doorway frames the figure to create a center of interest. The dark ceiling pushes our eye down and onto the figure. This work was created in pencil.

Materials

Pencil
Vinyl eraser
Black ink
#8 watercolor brush
Paper for ink
Water container
Paper towels

References

Draw from real life emphasizing value differences. Look at
- Gates
- Doorways
- Entryways
- Room interiors

LOOK BACK! Is the contrast of light areas against dark areas emphasized in the work so that a center of interest is created?

Lesson 1

UNIT 10
balance, symmetry

Vocabulary and Creative Exercise

SYMMETRY

IMPERFECT SYMMETRY

In *symmetry*, two sides mirror each other as in the above drawing after a watercolor by Heinrich Otto. Artists often use a type of *imperfect symmetry* in which they use similar objects on both sides, but not the same. In the art at the right, the bird's tail balances with the fruit hanging on the other side to create imperfect symmetry. This drawing is after a painting titled *Tropical Bird and Fruit* by an unknown American artist of the 1800's.

Be Creative

Much of the art you see is not drawn from direct observation. Imagination is an important element in art when the artist wants to get an idea across to someone else. Artists doing animation for movies use a combination of both observation and imagination. They first imagine scenes that fit the story line. They then observe real objects so that their objects have correct proportions and movements. They then must imagine how their character will look, often straying from the way it looks in real life. Their ability to use both observation and imagination effectively is what makes this type of art so enjoyable for the viewer.

Draw an illustration of a story or poem. First, imagine the scene. Next, gather references from photos or real life, of the type of characters or objects in the scene. Study these references to gather details. Draw a finished illustration.

OBJECTIVE: to use both observation and imagination in a finished work of art.

Lesson 2

Look at Symmetry in Art

Art Appreciation

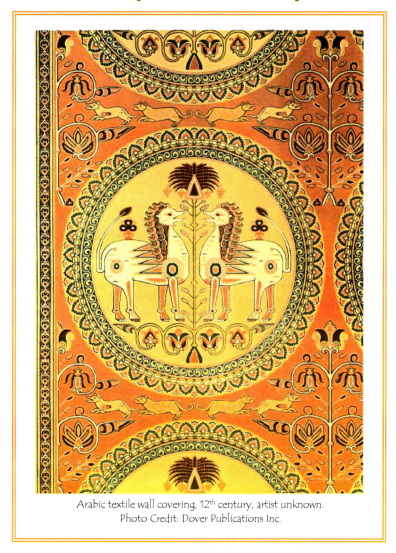

Arabic textile wall covering, 12th century, artist unknown.
Photo Credit: Dover Publications Inc.

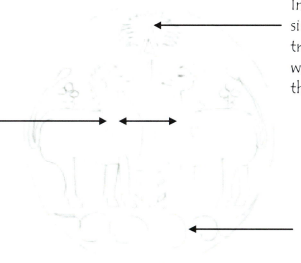

In perfect symmetry one side balances the other by showing two of the same object in reverse. This animal is shown reversed on the right side and facing the animal on the left.

In perfect symmetry a single object such as this tree is drawn as a shape with one side mirroring the opposite side.

Designs or patterns repeat and mirror each other in perfect symmetry.

53

The Culture
ANCIENT LITERATURE AND MATHEMATICS INSPIRE NEW ART

In the 7th and 8th centuries Muslim conquerors invaded Persia, Mesopotamia, Egypt, North Africa, and Spain. With this new religion came a strict rule that no images of any kind could be made. During this time a type of Renaissance took place at Baghdad, Iraq, where Muslims began translating ancient Greek and Latin manuscripts into the Arabic language. They discovered geometry in the writings. The ideas of geometry and the need for an art without identifiable images developed into an art of decorative patterns, called arabesques. This new art swept away any association to the real world or experiences people have in it. Since the design could be repeated and go on forever it symbolized the infinite nature of the Muslim god, Allah. Persian art is known for its patterns. Christian art of the same period, pulled heavily from this purely decorative approach too. Although they did not choose to eliminate images completely, they debated the issue for many centuries.

The Art
THE ARABESQUE

The **arabesque** is an elaborate design of repeating geometric forms that often echo the forms of plants and animals. Forbidden by their religion to reproduce any kind of subject matter including human figures, animals, or nature scenes, Islamic artists focused their ideas on creating elaborate patterns. Ancient Persian fabrics and tiles were the artistic outlet for these artists. The tiles were used in palaces and royal homes and stretched from the floor all the way onto arched ceilings. The rugs became treasured items not only in Iran but throughout the world. Arabic art designs are used today because of their bold, rich display of pattern.

Tile mosaics from a building in Kunya-Urgench and hall in Alhambra, Granada.
Photo Credit: Dover Publications Inc.

The Challenge

Create a pattern that is based on just a few design elements. Repeat the elements using symmetry. You may be familiar with this type of symmetry through American quilt patterns. Quilt patterns are based on the same ideas used by Arabic painters but originated because of a very different kind of restriction. Early Americans were poor and cloth was in high demand. People would cut the strongest parts from worn fabrics and piece them together in colorful patterns. It is interesting to note that both developments of pattern came through restrictions of some type. People are endlessly creative, even with restrictions, and desire to make beautiful things.

HOW TO ACHIEVE SYMMETRY

Lesson 3

Techniques

Perfect symmetry is seen in individual objects, but is not often seen in landscapes or groups of objects in the natural world. Below are examples of perfect symmetry. The bee and the face are the same on both sides.

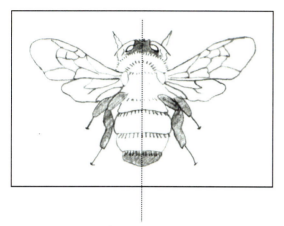

Artists most often arrange things using imperfect symmetry. Imperfect symmetry balances because the object on one side is similar in shape, size, or value to the object on the other side. Below, the fish balances with the boat because the close-up point of view makes them similar in size. The mountain peak balances with the group of trees creating an imperfect symmetry.

Try New Techniques

Draw an object or a scene that uses imperfect symmetry. Balance each side by using objects that are similar in weight, value, or size.

The Project

Lesson 4

Application

Do an imaginary drawing, using any type of subject matter. Think about balancing one side with the other using two objects with similarities. Decide whether your subject will best be shown using perfect symmetry or imperfect symmetry.

Student Gallery

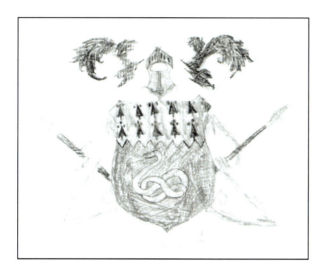

Student work: Symmetrical design (top) by Nathaniel Ellis, (below) by Katie Potts.

Materials

Pencil
Vinyl eraser
Black ink
#8 watercolor brush
Paper for ink
Water container
Paper towels

References

Use any reference that is appropriate to your imagined design. Artists often design from their imaginations, and then go to references for more accurate information to use in their drawings. We use information in a reference to make our drawings more accurate.

LOOK BACK! How is symmetry used to show balance in your design?

Lesson 1

UNIT 11
balance, asymmetry

In asymmetry, balance is achieved using dissimilar objects on each side. Balance occurs only when there is something on each side that pulls the eye towards it as in the drawing after a work by Johan Barthold Jongkind, titled *View of the Town of Maasluis*. Because the small figure is dark, it balances with the immense water mill on the opposite side, creating an asymmetrical composition.

Be Creative

Any subject is good for art making, but it takes input from the artist to put it on paper in an interesting way. Test your ability to make a very common object with little visual appeal become a source for art.

You will need at least 20 paper clips. The flat shape is not very interesting. Bend the paper clips into the most interesting shapes you can. These should be free standing shapes: shapes that stand up on their own. Once you do this, choose the most interesting shape and angle from which to view the paper clip. Draw a picture of it large enough to fill up the page. You may make it much larger than its actual size to create visual interest in the drawing. Draw three more pictures, changing the clips or the way that you draw them to add even more interest.

It is up to the artist to make objects interesting. If an object is boring and you cannot generate interest you need to change it somehow.

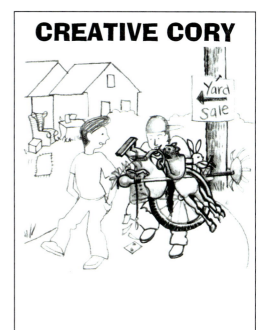

CREATIVE CORY

Sure, Cory, a buck for *all that* is a steal but...what ya gonna do with it?

OBJECTIVE: to learn to search for the most visually appealing aspects of a subject.

Lesson 2

Look at Asymmetry in Art

Art Appreciation

Chinese Cut-Paper Design, artist Unknown
Photo Credit: Dover Publications Inc.

The light outline of the mountains and cloud are not as heavy as the tree on the left, but are heavy enough to draw our eyes to this portion of the picture.

Heavy lines are used in this part of the picture. Our eyes are drawn to this side.

58

The Culture

THE CHINESE PREFERENCE FOR CURVED LINES

What ancient Chinese art might have looked like or what form it took is a bit of a mystery, but it is agreed on that the Song (Sung) dynasty (A.D.960-1279) was the classic period of Chinese painting. A type of perfection in line painting was reached during that period that influenced Chinese art from that point onward. These Eastern artists had a preference for curves. "When a Chinese artist had to represent a prancing horse, he seemed to fit it together out of a number of rounded shapes" (112 Gombrich). The beauty of a landscape, a draped figure, or an animal could be shown in lines that twist, turn, and flow in perfectly spaced rhythms, giving a sense of movement to the whole picture. The art is never overworked. Each mark is executed with freshness and exactness. The Chinese artist sacrifices particular details. He uses line to simplify the complex forms found in nature. A work consisting of curved lines sets the viewer at ease. It is not difficult to understand why Chinese artists choose this form as the form that describes beauty.

The Art

CUT-PAPER ART FORM

Chinese paper cutting has existed as a form of art for thousands of years. The invention of paper originated in China. Chinese legend tells that the new invention of paper was presented to the Emperor in the year 105 AD. The use of paper in Arabic nations and later European nations would not happen for another 700 years. Chinese nobles in royal palaces used paper cut designs for entertainment. Men could cut the elaborate designs freehand with a sharp scissors. From the 7th to 13th century, paper cutting became popular for decorating festivals. In the rural countryside of mainland China, girls were expected to gain the skill before marriage and display their skills to the family members of the suitor. Professional paper cutters also existed in China and worked in shops. The Chinese made folded paper forms in the first and second centuries. These forms were introduced to Japan in the sixth century and are now referred to by their Japanese name, origami. In origami forms of animals, birds, cups, and designs are folded from small pieces of square paper. Paper plays an important role in Chinese arts and crafts.

The Challenge

Study how the artist used both line and filled in shapes to create the asymmetrical design in the landscape on the previous page. With pencil, draw an asymmetrical landscape of your own. Decide which parts will remain line and which part s will be filled in. Once the design is created in pencil and reworked until you like it, then use ink and brush to make a bold black design.

HOW TO SEE MORE ACCURATELY BY FOCUSING ON NEGATIVE SPACE

Lesson 3 — Techniques

Sometimes when drawing an object our mind gets in the way of what we are really seeing. We draw what we think the object looks like instead of drawing the shapes that are there. One way to see how the shapes of the object relate to each other is to look at the negative spaces. Negative space is what is around, behind, or between the object. When we force our minds to focus on the negative spaces or "empty" spaces it may take a while for the space to pop into focus. We are asking ourselves to look at nothing, the space that isn't a thing. These negative spaces create shapes of their own.

To most easily see negative space, set up a subject against a wall so that there aren't distractions or "things" in the background. These drawings are most fun when working with ink directly. That way one can fully concentrate on working in the moment and is not concerned with erasing or making corrections. Once you are ready to begin, paint the negative spaces. In this situation the wall would be negative.

Positive and negative spaces are focused on in this picture of a drum set. The asymmetry is from the top of the painting to the bottom. The large negative space of black at the top is balanced by the smaller black spot in the lower part of the picture.

Try New Techniques

Draw a picture of the negative space around an object. There may be many of these negative shapes. Help your viewer see these shapes by shading in the areas. If you had fun with this method of drawing, do a second drawing with two objects and use ink for more dramatic effect.

The Project

Lesson 4 — Application

Choose an object with many parts or choose a group of objects. Balance the picture, paying attention to placement of the objects and their values. Choose an asymmetrical arrangement.

Student Gallery

Student Alex Unrein used a model boat and a lighthouse as references and then added water to the scene. Dark values in each object and the bottom wave pull our eye in those directions.

Student work: by Laura Freeman. The dogs' heads create an asymmetrical balance.

Materials

Pencil
Vinyl eraser
Black ink
#8 watercolor brush
Paper for ink
Water container
Paper towels

References

You may use any source of reference needed to draw a picture of something you are interested in. References come from the following places:
- Works of art
- Photographs
- Real life

LOOK BACK! Did you use asymmetry in the picture? How does your picture show asymmetry?

Lesson 1

UNIT 12
rhythm

Vocabulary and Creative Exercise

Repeating any element within a picture makes rhythm. The eye follows the elements and moves through the space of the picture. The tree trunks have repeated line, light value, and dark value in the spots. The eye follows the trunks across the picture after a work by Thoru Mabuchi, titled *Mountain Lake*.

Be Creative

Movie producers and fiction writers create new worlds for viewers and readers to explore. The movie producer creates models of these worlds while the writer uses words and relies on how the reader interprets them. The artist can create new worlds on paper. These new worlds are based on observations of the world we all know and see. The real world inspires us. It influences our imaginations.

Draw two pictures. One titled, "The World I See", where you draw observations of some part of the real world. The second titled, "The World I Create", where you use imagination to invent new things.

If you like to build things, you can create a model of the new world in a 3-dimentional-paper construction. Using plain paper, cut, paste, fold, and tape a part of your world on a base made from cardboard.

CREATIVE CORY

I think Cory's "New World" is encroaching on our old one.

OBJECTIVE: to use imagination while drawing from things found in the real world.

Lesson 2

Look at Rhythm in Art

Art Appreciation

Vincent van Gogh wanted people to feel something from the colors he chose. Here the eerie green color gives us a feeling of hopelessness or dread. He uses other devices to suggest the prisoner's conditions. The walls on the right and left lead us into the picture, but like the prisoners lives, lead only to another dead-end wall. They are trapped. The circle formed by the exercise line also suggests lives that do not go anywhere or accomplish things. Heads hang down and shoulders are slumped.

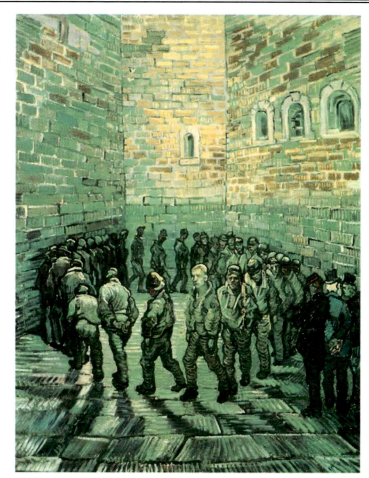

Vincent Van Gogh, *The Prison Exercise Yard*, 1890.
Photo Credit: Dover Publications Inc.

Rhythm helps the eye to move through the painting as it follows these repeated elements. Look at the arrows that show rhythm in the following places:

- Along the windows
- Down the bricks
- Around the prisoners
- Across the floor in the foreground
- Up the left side

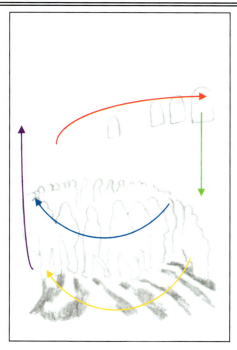

63

The Culture
EUROPEAN ART OF THE 20TH CENTURY

While Eastern tradition emphasized expressiveness through a traditional method of creating brush strokes just like the masters, the West in the 20th century would argue that one could not be expressive while following the path of another. Western artists redefined expressiveness as absolute originality. Artists had to become inventors (435 Gombrich). In the search for the next new idea the artist left behind traditional methods and techniques. Art training soon deteriorated. Lessons in how to paint were abandoned while creativity and original ideas were elevated as all important. This need for something new lead to distortions. At first the public was horrified by the changes brought about by Impressionism, Expressionism, Cubism, and a host of other "isms." These new ideas seemed to be a fitting way to express how people felt about the horrific events like the World Wars and revolutions that were taking place in the twentieth century. Art that reflected the events of the times used harsh colors directly from tubes of paint. Brush strokes became slashes that overpowered subject matter. People lost touch with the strong Christian heritage that pervaded art from 300 A.D. to 1800 A.D., so art was no longer used to show "beauty" and traditional morality. Art showed the immediate experience of a people who had lost their beliefs in ideas like morality, rightness, goodness, and truth. While not all people or art fits into this category, it is the general direction of thought in the twentieth century.

The Artist

Vincent van Gogh
(1853 – 1890)
DUTCH POST IMPRESSIONIST PAINTER

Although Vincent Van Gogh worked from nature, meaning that he looked at real objects as he painted them, he did not try to imitate it or make it look real. Instead of coloring a thing as it was, he explored the power of color to suggest a mood, an emotion, or a state of being. In describing his idea for a painting of his own bedroom, he says, "…Color is to do everything… is to be suggestive here of rest or of sleep in general. In a word, to look at the picture ought to rest the brain…" The harsh green of the prison painting on the previous page could suggest the harsh situation the prisoners found themselves in. The color makes us uncomfortable. Van Gogh, along with others of his time, would create new aims for art. No longer would photographic representation be the goal of the artist.

The Challenge

Imagine a scene with a group of figures that sets up a rhythm. You might get ideas from parades, marching bands, ball games, check-out lines in stores, or anywhere that people form lines. Make a drawing that shows motion and rhythm.

HOW TO CONTAIN MOVEMENT

Lesson 3

Techniques

Choosing a view to draw from can be a difficult assignment. There are often too many small objects, too many colors, and too many details in one scene. One does not need to include all of what they see when looking at a real scene. When drawing from nature, emphasize the big shapes. Sometimes these shapes have to be changed or modified to work with the picture space. In the first example, the tree trunk leads the eye out of the picture. The sun and the path do the same.

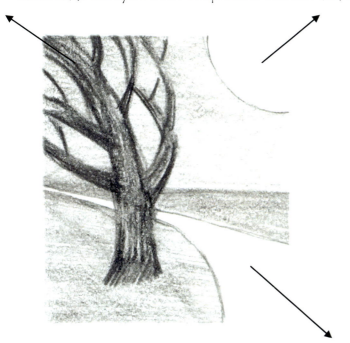
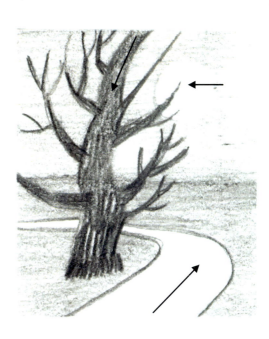

OUTWARD MOMEMENT   INWARD MOVEMENT

Watch the corners. If your picture is designed so that it takes the eye **out of** the corners, then people cannot stay interested in the picture for long. Arrange the objects so that the lines lead the eye **into** the picture. The shapes have been modified in the second picture so that the eye stays within the picture space. The tree leans inward. The sun is brought completely into the picture. The path leads in toward the viewer. These adjustments to the big shapes will work to keep the viewer interested even when small details are added.

Try New Techniques

Choose a scene from outdoors to draw. Draw in the big shapes first. Check to see that all the big shapes lead the eye inward, not outward. Change them if you need to. Then complete the picture with any details that you want to add. Draw the arrangement in pencil or in ink.

The Project

Lesson 4 — Application

Look for rhythm in a view of the home or out of doors. Look for repeated shapes, repeated lines, or other repeated elements in the scene. Show these in an ink drawing. You can exaggerate and change what you actually see to bring out certain rhythms.

Student Gallery

Student work is by Lavender Huskey and shows rhythm in the bricks, windows, and doorway shapes. It keeps our eye within the picture space by stopping the eye on the left and the right with a fence on one side and a bush on the other.

Materials

Black ink
Paper for ink
Pen holder and nib
Water container
Paper towel

References

Find a view from within the home or an out of doors scene that shows rhythm.

LOOK BACK! Did you use rhythm in the drawing? What elements are repeated?

Lesson 1

space without depth
UNIT 13

The space of the paper is filled with lines and shapes. How the artist uses those lines and shapes determines whether the viewer is aware of depth or distance. Here there is little depth. The flowers that sit behind the girl seem to pop out in front of her because white objects tend to jump forward and darker objects tend to recede. The striped shirt and stripes of the leaves seem to be at the same distance.
-Drawn after a work by Okiie Hashimoto, titled, *Young Woman and Iris*.

Be Creative

A common approach to making art is to find a suitable subject to draw and then proceed with little thought or inspiration. This is not the best method for making art that is truly inspiring. We challenge you to reverse the beginning process. Instead of searching for a subject, let the subject find you. First make a change in your surroundings. Go somewhere that is very different from where you usually make art. If you are able to go to a park, field, wooded area, or across the street, do so. If you can only go to your yard, sit on a side of the house or in a corner of the yard that you do not usually sit in. Do not try to come up with images right away. Sit and wait. Let your mind wander. Slowly take in sights and sounds and weather. Wait until you see something new you would like to draw or until ideas happen. Let the subject come to you.

Draw a picture of the thing that captures your interest. Begin drawing only after taking time to fully absorb your new surroundings.

CREATIVE CORY

Said he was inspired by his trip to the zoo.
What do they keep in those places these days?

OBJECTIVE: to allow time for observation and imagination, leading to inspiration.

Lesson 2

Look at "Space without Depth" in Art

Art Appreciation

Aboriginal bark painting, depicting kangaroos and a fork-tongued lizard. These images are made with a mixture of ochre and natural pigments. Bark. Aboriginal art. Location: Private Collection, Prague, Czech Republic
Photo Credit: Werner Forman / Art Resource, NY

Some paintings appear more flat than others. When art has a purpose beyond just looking like the subject matter, it is usually beneficial to eliminate the things that would detract from that purpose. The highly patterned interior of the animals and canoe, which only the Aboriginal Australian artists know the purpose of, make the objects appear flat. The solid background also helps to create an image with little depth.

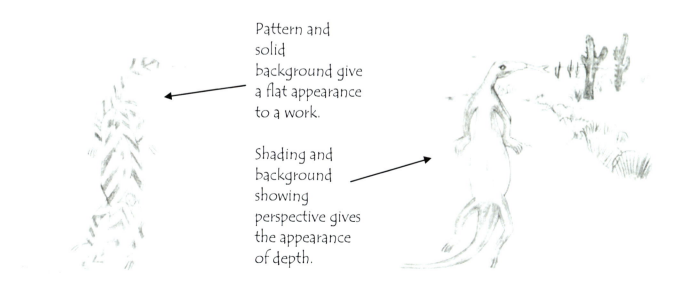

Pattern and solid background give a flat appearance to a work.

Shading and background showing perspective gives the appearance of depth.

68

The Culture
ABORIGINAL AUSTRALIANS

Those Australians who originally lived in Australia are called Aboriginal Australians or Indigenous Australians. Britain colonized the continent in 1788. Many Australians died within months, as often happened when Europeans first contacted indigenous peoples. This was due to the spread of European diseases that Australians were not immune to. The Aboriginal Australians had a story of creation that they called the dreamtime. The dreamtime is thought to be connected to both the time of creation and their current dreams. They have several characters for god, and his son, and these are depicted in their art. There is also a rainbow serpent, which often appears in the art. One version of the creation story tells that a huge serpent traveled over the land leaving tracks. It called for two frogs that were full of water. The rainbow snake tickled them and as they laughed the water came out of their mouths and filled the tracks. That is how the rivers were formed. These beliefs and others of the dreamtime are represented in bark paintings.

The Art
ABORIGINAL PAINTING

In Australia, artists paint on tree bark. They use only white and red paint, which are different in value and stand out well against each other. Their process of making a painting is unique. They first cut the bark off the tree in a large rectangular chunk with a steel ax. At one time they used a stone to do this. Next they straighten and cure the bark. They cover the entire piece of bark with a natural red pigment made from rock. Using tiny blades of grass as brushes, they paint in the white lines. The white areas are light in value and the animal shapes stand out well against a dark background. The work is put into a fire to finish it. This work may at first look simplified, but on taking a closer look we see that it is complex. The Aboriginal Australian artist omits all the unimportant elements and details which don't add to the idea he is working with, just as designers do today. He is not drawing animals and canoes as he sees them, but is extracting the parts of those things that fit the purpose of his work. Simplicity in art is not bad. Designers today simplify visual means to get across specific ideas. We know that Aboriginal art has a religious function, but the content of it is unknown. Meanings are kept secret and passed down from man to man within the tribe. The animals seem to have certain organs showing. The other marks do not relate to the skeleton or muscles, and seem to be pattern related to nothing we know about the insides of animals, nor their outsides. In this way their painting remains a mystery.

The Challenge

Look for patterns in nature. The rings of a tree stump, the spiral design of a shell, or the fan pattern of a leaf are some examples of patterns. Draw the object in simplified form. Use lines that emphasize the pattern and disregard color or other elements that might detract from the pattern. Make several attempts of playing with the pattern until you have a design you like. It may no longer resemble the original object once it has been modified several times.

HOW TO USE PEN AND INK

Lesson 3 — Techniques

Many artists like the fine, crisp lines that are obtained with pen and ink. Pen work also has the advantage of reproducing well using a copy machine or scanner.

To begin, press your pen nib into the penholder. Different nibs make different marks. We have suggested a fine nib be used first. Add to your collection, as you like. Wash the nib to remove the coating of oil often left by the manufacturer. To clean pen points after use, rub your hands with soap and then rub the nibs with soapy fingers. Rinse the soap off and dry the pen points with a piece of lint-free cloth. If you get careless and let the ink dry in the nib, use ammonia to remove it. Store with the point up!

Dip the pen into the ink just above the reservoir. Do not dip it up to the handle. The reservoir is the hole cut into the top of the nib. It holds ink so one can work longer before dipping back into the bottle. Slide the underside of the pen along the neck of the bottle to remove excess ink. Always use scrap paper, testing strokes before laying them down on paper.

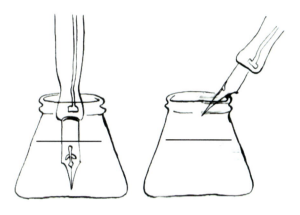

Make a variety of marks with the pen filling a page with different strokes. Work from light to dark and from thick to thin with the pointed nib.

Try New Techniques

Draw a picture using ink and pen. Practice making thin and thick strokes by varying the pressure slightly on the pen. Do not press so hard that you permanently spread the points of the nib apart. Draw things you are familiar with or have drawn before. Drawing familiar things can help you to be successful right away with the new materials.

The Project

Lesson 4 — Application

Choose a favorite photo or work from real life. Compose a picture that shows space with little depth. Look for areas of difference so that you can use variations in line to show those differences.

Student Gallery

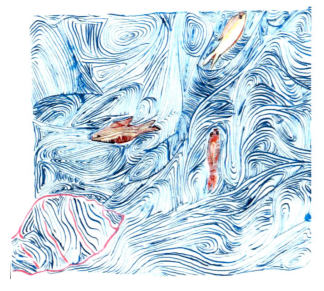

Materials

Pencil
Vinyl eraser
Black ink
Ink pen
Brush
Paper for Ink
Water container
Paper towels

References

Photographs make good references. Choose animals or subjects with textures that allow you to experiment with mark making. If inspired, you can work from real life.

Student work by Ryan MacDonald, above, takes a close up point of view showing little depth. He uses variations in line and some brush work.

Ariel Ellis works directly from life in this colored ink work showing a space with little depth. If you like working with ink, you may want to purchase a few colors to work with.

LOOK BACK! What details did you show in the picture? How did you show space with little depth?

Lesson 1

space with depth
UNIT 14

Depth refers to seeing in the distance. Depth is shown in the three groups of travelers because their sizes change, becoming smaller as they go further into the distance.

Drawn after an etching by James McBey titled, *Dawn, Camel Patrol.*

Be Creative

Sometimes it is easier to understand a concept if you work with it for awhile. This assignment will help you discover what objects look like as they move into the distance. Choose three objects that are the same in height such as three cups, three dolls, three action figures, or three baseballs. Arrange and rearrange these objects on a table.

Draw the arrangements in three ways as follows:
1. Place the three objects side by side. Make a quick sketch of them.
2. Arrange the objects differently, this time closer together, so that they overlap as seen from your position. Make a quick sketch of this arrangement.
3. Arrange the objects with one close to you, the other near the middle, and the last near the far end of the table. Make a quick sketch of this arrangement.

Now evaluate the results. What differences do you see? Look for the same kinds of overlapping, size changes, and changes in position the next time you sit at the dinner table. The table is full of objects, many the same in size, but how do they look from your position? How would you show that in a drawing?

OBJECTIVE: to explore and discover what objects look like as they move into the distance.

Lesson 2

Looking at "Space With Depth" in Art

Art Appreciation

High on the picture plane. The picture plane is the flat surface of the paper. The top part of the paper is high. The bottom part of the plane is low.

Low on the picture

Kuniyoshi (1797-1861); View of Mt. Fuji on a Clear Day from off Tsukuda, c. 1843.
Photo Credit: Dover Publications Inc.

Depth is shown in the distant mountain by making it small and raising it on the picture plane. We know that the boat on the left is closer to us than the net because it sits lower on the picture plane. We know that the net is closer than the boat on the right because it overlaps and it is lower on the picture plane. Depth is also shown in the size of the boats. Depth is shown in the angles of the lines chosen to represent the boat.

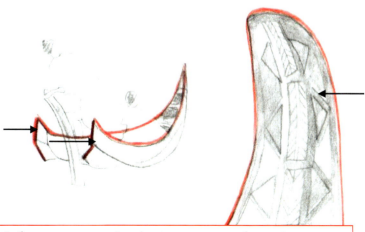

To show depth with an object such as this boat, we see that it is built of complex angles and curves which mimic each other on each side.

The view of a canoe, painted by the Aboriginal Australian artist, and shown in the last unit, is a simple outline viewed from above. It does not consist of complicated angles. If one did view a canoe from above it would have symmetrical sides. The way the tip curves to the left suggests a curve of a canoe but is not related to actual visual information.

The boat on the left suggests depth. The boat copied from the Aborigines bark painting, seen in the previous unit, does not.

73

Art History

The Culture
JAPANESE UKIYO-E PRINTS

Ukiyo-e is a type of Japanese woodblock print produced from the 17th to 20th centuries. Ukiyo-e means "pictures of the floating world". These pictures featured landscapes and the activities centering on Japanese theatre. The young artists who started Ukiyo-e painting did not follow Japanese traditional painting styles but were individualists following their own desires and tastes. They incorporated European ideas of perspective and their paintings began to show depth or distance in European rather than Oriental ways. The prints were first produced for books, as illustrations, and then the popularity of their work led to the demand for single prints. A type of postcard was created for metropolitan customers of Edo, now called Tokyo, in the 1650's. These woodblock prints were made in black ink and then colored in by hand. The common people of Japan could afford them and loved them. As technology developed in the 1800's they were able to print these cards in full color and the demand grew even higher throughout all of Japan and some made their way to European nations. Subjects included courtesans, sumo wrestlers and popular actor's portraits. Landscapes included common people within a vast landscape and often Mount Fuji can be seen in the background.

The Artist
Utagawa Kuniyoshi (1798-1861)
Japanese Ukiyo-e Printmaker

Young Yoshisaburo, later called Utagawa Kuniyoshi, was the son of a silk-dyer. He assisted his father by making designs for textiles using rich colors. People noticed his talent for drawing and he was soon able to work as an apprentice for the famous print master Utagawa Toyokuni. He soon became a chief pupil in the studio. Kuniyoshi experienced times of success and times when it was difficult to produce the numbers of prints needed to sustain his career. Reforms were announced in the years of 1841-1843, which restricted public displays of luxury items. Prints of courtesans and actors were included in this government ban. Kuniyoshi began producing caricature prints, what we know of as comics, during this time. They symbolically criticized the government, but were outside of the restrictions. He also produced landscapes using Western perspective. Kuniyoshi taught many pupils that went on to become masters of the Utagawa School.

The Challenge

Draw a picture with many objects and show depth by overlapping objects. Draw **through** the objects so that lines connect in the right places. These lines can be erased later.

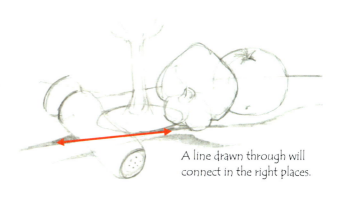

A line drawn through will connect in the right places.

HOW TO SHOW DEPTH

Lesson 3

Techniques

Depth is shown using several methods. These methods work together to convince the viewer of distance in the artwork. The methods are OVERLAP, DIMINISHED SIZE, and CHANGE IN POSITION.

Depth is shown when one object overlaps another. One person is clearly seen as being behind the other.

As figures go into the distance, they become smaller.

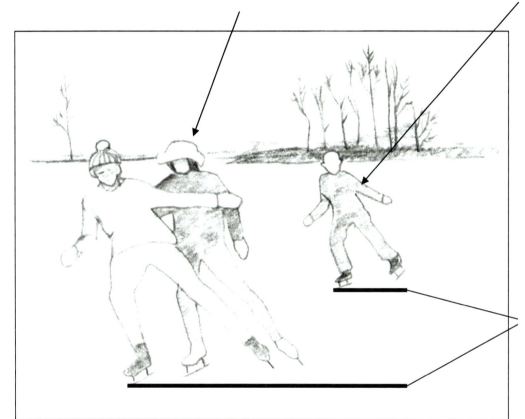

Show depth by positioning the people closest to the viewer nearer the bottom of the page, while the one further in the distance is positioned higher on the page.

Try New Techniques

Practice drawing objects that overlap. Set up or observe some objects that overlap. Notice where the lines overlap. Be careful not to change your posture as you draw. If you move, the positions of the objects and where they overlap appear to move.

The Project

Lesson 4 — Application

Go outdoors and look for scenes with depth. Draw the type of landscape that you see around you. Notice overlapping, the diminishing size of objects, and where these objects meet the ground. Draw the scene and then finish it in ink.

Student Gallery

Student Work: by Dan Ellis (cir. 1974). The bridge is closest so it is positioned at the bottom of the page. The buildings are further away and smaller. Mountains in the background are most distant so less detail is shown. The hills in the foreground overlap the buildings behind. The buildings then overlap the hills behind them.

Materials

Pencil
Vinyl eraser
Black ink
Ink pen
Paper for Ink
Water container
Paper towels

References

Draw an outdoor scene where you can see depth.

LOOK BACK! Did you show depth in the drawing by using overlap, diminishing size, or a change in position on the paper?

Lesson 1

UNIT 15
perspective

Vocabulary and Creative Exercise

A formula for drawing vertical or horizontal lines as they go into the distance is called perspective. The horizontal lines of the edge of the road converge as they go into the distance. The vertical lines are parallel to the sides of the paper. This work is drawn after a woodcut by Hermann Paul titled, *Promenades*.

Be Creative

When you imagine, take time and let your mind wander. Images will come to mind if other things do not distract you. Close your eyes. Keep paper and pencil beside you. Once you have an image, get it on paper as a rough sketch. Make several rough sketches. Once the imagination stage is done, choose an image you like and make a finished drawing from it.

Images from the imagination are often inspired by something one sees in the real world. Briefly observe a neighbor's house or nearby building. Look at the details. Is it neat with flowers and a perfect lawn or an abandoned, boarded up area? What do you imagine is inside? Draw a picture of the front door, opened, and what you might see inside.

OBJECTIVE: to observe details and use them as a starting point for the imagination.

Lesson 2

Look at Perspective in Art

Art Appreciation

Camille Pissarro (1830-1903); *Place du Théâtre Français, Paris: Rain*; 1898
Photo Credit : Dover Publications Inc.

Once people began to show depth in their paintings, it was noticed that objects with straight edges, like buildings or streets, did not seem to line up right. It was as if these objects were each being viewed from different angles instead of from the same point of view. Artists began to place a single point in the painting from which all objects would line up with. This is called a vanishing point and it is a point that lies on the horizon line. The horizon line is a line where the earth meets the sky. Perspective is a technique for showing distance based on the optical illusion that parallel lines seem to converge as they recede toward a vanishing point.

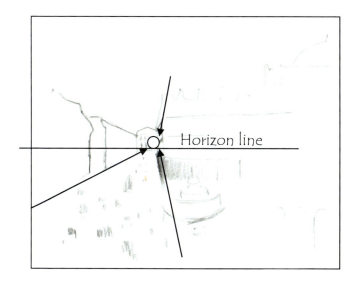

The parallel sides of the street converge at the vanishing point.

78

Art History

The Culture
THE ADVANTAGE OF VANISHING POINT PERSPECTIVE

It may seem that all of our modern ideas about how to paint began with the European Renaissance and to some degree that is true. The theory of vanishing point perspective was one of those ideas. It was developed by the architect Filippo Brunelleschi (1377-1446) and published by Alberti in *On Painting* in 1435. Not only did the discovery influence painting, but also inspired new theatre designs and was used on flats for theatrical backdrops (Jacobus 263). It was a perfect way to add depth to a flat surface. This was a much needed device for expanding imaginary space on the stage. An artist, painting 400 years later, was interested in showing off the newly built city streets of Paris, France. He naturally chose to use this wonderful theory to organize his painting of city life. Pissarro painted this view and thirty-two others from the window of a hotel room. It overlooks the Théâtre Français. He painted this damp winter day with its overcast skies in the colors he saw. He enjoyed painting these works and said, "… I am delighted to be able to do these Parisian streets which people usually call ugly, but which are so silvery, so luminous, and so vital." We still use vanishing point perspective today.

The Artist
Camille Pissarro (1830-1903) French Impressionist Painter

Camille Pissarro was the oldest of his fellow Impressionists and was the primary developer of the Impressionist technique. This technique was the most dramatic move away from traditional art that had ever been seen up to that time. He used a bright color palette. He encouraged others to do the same and to avoid using black. He encouraged them to paint in "dabs" and so he developed a quick style that allowed them to get many colors on the canvas so that the moment could be captured. He was also very fond of working out of doors. His lively personality allowed him to be a friend and influence on some of the most difficult personalities of that time, including Edgar Degas, Paul Cézanne, and Paul Gauguin. He has been called the Father of Impressionism because of the great influence he had on that movement. Pissarro exhibited at all eight of the Impressionist exhibitions.

The Challenge

Draw perspective lines over the picture on the right. Compare the perspective lines in Pissarro's painting of a Paris street to those in this painting of a village street, called *Marizy Sainte-Genevieve*, by Maurice Utrillo. The village wall (white) slumps and the red wall and houses do not follow the perspective line. These adaptations from exact perspective make the village an interesting subject to paint. Find an interesting location in your area and draw it using one point perspective.

Photo Credit: Dover Publications Inc.

HOW TO DRAW PERSPECTIVE

Lesson 3

Techniques

Draw a horizon line across the page with a straight edge. Next, draw a vanishing point somewhere on the horizon line. All perspective lines will go to the vanishing point. They can be used to mark the tops and bottoms of objects like trees, buildings, or the edges of parallel lines seen in roads or railroad tracks.

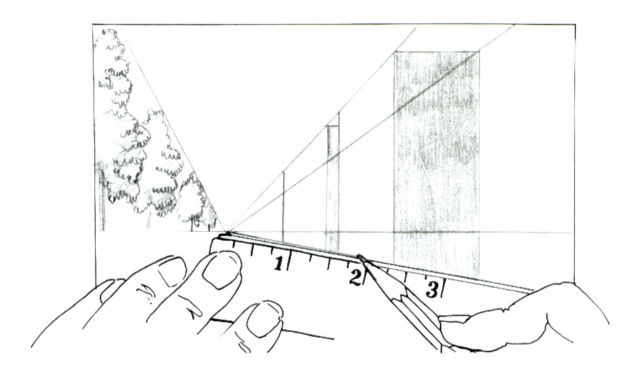

To find out more about using perspective, look in technical books on perspective. Look for the terms linear perspective, one point perspective, or two-point perspective. You can also search for information on the web.

Try New Techniques

Draw a picture using perspective as shown above. Include imagined objects that are cubed, round, and free-formed objects like the trees, within the drawing.

The Project

Lesson 4 — Application

Draw a scene using perspective lines. These scenes can be found by standing along a straight street with a row of buildings. In the painting below the road is curved rather than straight, but still the sides of the road get closer together. Perspective lines, whether straight or curved, narrow toward the horizon line as the road goes into the distance.

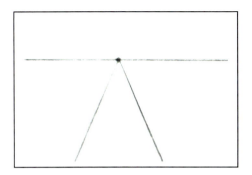
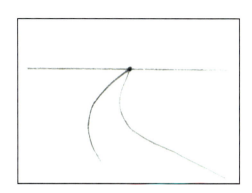

Student Gallery

Student Work: by James Oltmans

Materials

Pencil
Vinyl eraser
Black ink
Ink pen and brush
Paper for Ink
Water container
Paper towels

References

Look in your own neighborhood for perspective lines. Observe an outdoor scene from a window or outdoors.

LOOK BACK! Did you use perspective to show parallel lines as they go into the distance?

Lesson 1

UNIT 16
proportion

Proportion of the figure is the measurement of the parts of the body or how the parts relate to each other. This work is drawn after an etching by Jean-Francois Millet titled, *Going Out to Work*.

Be Creative

To ask, "How do I draw a nose?" or "How do I draw a flower?" misses the point of making art. These questions assume that one nose is like another or that one flower is like another. In fact, each nose, flower, or any other natural object is distinctly different from others. Diversity is part of the complex world we live in. Not only is each object different, but it looks different depending on the angle we view it from.

When you draw, think about specific things. Ask, "What does Grandpa's nose look like in profile?" or "What do the petals of this lily look like when facing the sun?" One must look at these specific objects for the answers. Therefore, the real question becomes, "How do I draw the shapes, forms, and areas of shading that I see?"

Draw a picture showing the details of what you see.

OBJECTIVE: to see the true object in all its unique qualities, not the symbol to represent it. To see how the object changes in appearance when viewed from different angles.

CREATIVE CORY

Hey, I like Cory's flower. It looks different. What's he know that we don't?

"Draw something specific or particular rather than something general."

Lesson 2
Look at Proportion in Art

Art Appreciation

Eishi, Japanese Printmaker, *The Courtesan Hinazuru of Choji-ya*, c. mid 1790's. Photo Credit: Dover Publications Inc.

Guy Rose, American Impressionist, *The Green Parasol*, 1909. Photo Credit: Dover Publications Inc.

Proportion is a matter of taste. We find different proportions used for the human figure in different countries and at different times. In China and Japan bodies tend to be elongated with hands and feet proportionately small. Notice in the Eastern painting that the eyes are placed 3/4th the way between the chin to the top of the head. Whether standing or sitting, Japanese figures sweep into a curve. All the body parts are rounded. Do you see a difference in the painting at the right? Even though both women are dressed in Japanese attire, the one on the right is clearly painted by a Western artist. This painting is by an American Impressionist. The Impressionists were greatly influenced by Japanese art and costume. This artist has used Western proportion. The eyes are half way between the chin and top of the head. The figure almost looks flattened or squashed when compared to the Japanese figure.

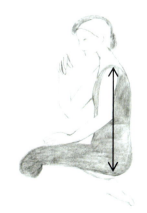

By connecting the body parts we see in the painting, we can get a good idea of the proportions of each figure. The Japanese figure is much more slender, stretched, than the American figurer.

83

The Cultures

EAST AND WEST AND WHY WE MAKE ART

To really understand a work of art it is helpful to know the goals of the artist. We should ask why the art was made. European and American art of the twentieth century was created in a race to see who could show us the next new change. Art was praised more for its novelty than for its quality of craftsmanship. Rather than being praised for gaining fine skills like one's teacher, artists were praised for individuality and being radically different from ones teacher. This emphasis on originality can lead to many improvements in life. It can also leave us without direction or purpose. Art became, at this time, about the individual experience and did not necessarily reflect the experiences of anyone else. It lost its importance in society. Much of the work was very poorly made. The idea of "originality" as the guide for judging works of art is purely a Western idea. As Gombrich writes in *The Story of Art*, "many ages and many parts of the globe knew nothing of this obsession. The craftsman who made the beautiful rug... would have been surprised to be asked to invent a new pattern never seen before." See the Persian rug on page 53. He goes on to say that the artist had in mind "making a fine rug" and wouldn't it be nice if this attitude was more widespread in Western society today. The Eastern artist still makes beautiful paintings. "Beauty", as it developed through the use of line, pattern, and color, is still a part of what a work of art is. Since beauty was not a goal of the most celebrated twentieth century Western artists, ugliness, emptiness, or futility were possible themes. Art could then look bad and still be exalted. Some think the answer to bad art is to control what people can make, what subject matter they can choose, and how they represent it. Socialist and communist governments have controlled artistic output in the past and some countries still do today. This government control has not led to good work or work of any importance. The problem of bad art must be approached as individuals. We each need to look at art and rethink the reasons for making it. When individuals value worthwhile ideals, it will show in the art they make and the high quality of that art. When you look at a work of art in a museum, consider your response. Do you like it? Why or why not? Was it made in Eastern societies or Western societies? How does that affect the way you look at the work? What time period was it made in and what was going on in the world at that time? What were the ideas the artist was working with? Was he searching for a truer realism? Was he interested in beauty? Did his culture see beauty in curved lines or realistic form? Did the artist take a modern Western approach and create the work in order to be new, original, shocking, or rebellious? Asking questions like these will help you understand the art you encounter. We also hope it will encourage you to consider choosing good reasons to make art. Many of those reasons can be discovered in artworks of the past. We hope you've picked up a few good ideas as you've explored art around the world and that you use them in your own work.

The Challenge

Compare the two works on the previous page. Which appeals to you more? Draw the figure shown in one of the paintings. Look for shapes and other elements of art. Copying a painting makes us more aware of the artist's choices. That is why copying a work of fine art is of value. We CAN learn from the masters.

HOW TO MEASURE THE FIGURE

Lesson 3
Techniques

Keep proportion in mind when you draw the figure. There are many ways to measure the proportions of the body. Many divide the body into head heights, but those lines do not line up with other parts of the body. This illustration is most useful because it does line up with so many parts that we can identify and remember.

The torso is the largest area. Notice that the waist is centered in the middle of the torso on the male and female.

Notice the major points on the body.
A- top of head to shoulder blades
B- base of the neck to waist
C- waist to crotch
D- crotch to knees
E- knees to ankles
F- just above the ankles

The distances between A and B equals the distance between B and C, C and D, D and E, and E and F.

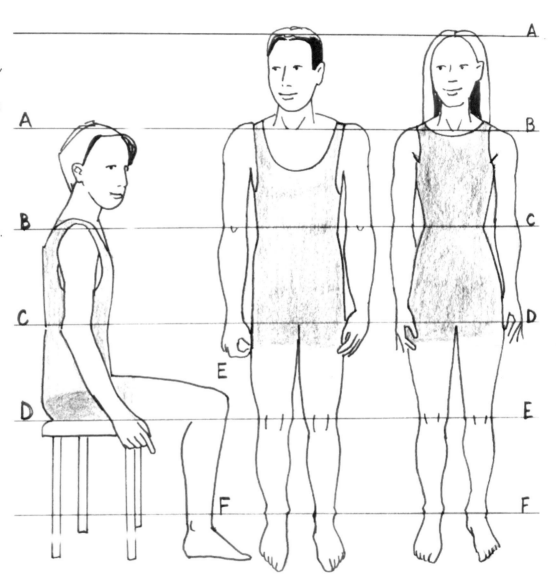

Look for the same points in the seated figure. Notice how the leg joins the torso. Notice how the torso is thinner from the side.

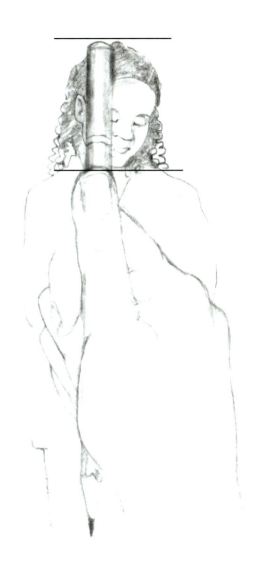

MEASURE PROPORTIONS
To check that you draw a figure in proportion, you can measure the figure you are looking at. Hold your arm out straight, with the pencil in your hand. Line up the pencil to the top of the head then mark with your thumbnail at the chin. Compare this measurement to another area of the body, keeping the thumb in place.

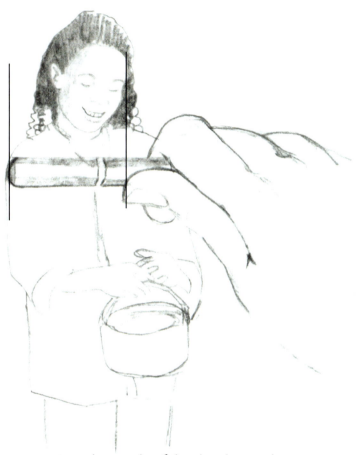

The length of the head is measured. It is then compared to the width of the shoulders. The shoulders are wider than the head is long and the artist can draw it that way on the paper. The measurement lines up with the shoulder to the side of the face. Many more measurements and comparisons can be made in this way. Always view the subject from the same angle and direction, keeping your posture erect. Always hold your arm out straight so the distance of the pencil to your eye remains consistent.

Try New Techniques

Draw a diagram of a figure you have found in a photograph. Compare the measurements to those on the previous page. In a second drawing, work from real life. Use the method of measuring shown on this page.

The Project

Lesson 4 — Application

Draw a figure keeping proportions in mind as you draw. Notice the variety of lines used in this drawing. You might add interest by placing your figure in a setting and showing what is around the figure.

Student Gallery

This student work by Amy Wright was drawn from a photograph.

Materials

Pencil
Vinyl eraser
Black ink
Ink pen or brush
Paper for Ink
Water container
Paper towels

References

Use any type of reference you prefer. Draw a figure or several figures from a photograph, a work of fine art, or from imagination.

LOOK BACK! Is the work well proportioned? Does your drawing show a figure in a setting?

Evaluation Sheet
For Obtaining a Number and Letter Grade

Teachers may calculate a number and letter grade for each project within each unit. Follow the instructions below when reviewing the final work. DO NOT take off points for concepts not yet taught. Follow the objectives carefully when grading.

Because of art's subjective qualities it is best to mark higher rather than lower when deciding between two levels of achievement. If the student enjoys doing the lessons and has made the effort to create a work of art in a thoughtful way, then that student should be given a good grade. Allow the student to grow into mature artistic expression. Do not demand results that can only be obtained by years of experience that the student has not yet had. It is very likely that an individual who enjoys making art will get A's. This does not mean that the student has arrived at a full knowledge and use of artistic concepts. It does mean the student is doing well in the pursuit of that goal.

LEVELS OF ACHIEVEMENT: Choose one number of points that most accurately describes the work from each of the three categories below. Add the numbers from categories 1, 2, 3, and 4. This is the student's total score for the unit. This number can be translated into a letter grade: 90-100 (A), 80-89 (B), 70-79 (C), Uncompleted work (D-F).

1. Creative Exercise	2. The Challenge	3. Technique Drawing	4. The Project
25 POINTS/ COMPLETED ASSIGNMENT OBTAINING ALL OBJECTIVES IN THE GREEN BOX	25 POINTS/ COMPLETED ASSIGNMENT SHOWING GOOD UNDERSTANDING OF CONCEPT SHOWN IN ART WORK	25 POINTS/ COMPLETED ASSIGNMENT SHOWING A GOOD UNDERSTANDING AND USE OF MATERIALS OR TECHNIQUES	25 POINTS/ COMPLETED PROJECT SHOWING A GOOD UNDERSTANDING OF THE UNIT (SEE TITLE) AND USE OF THOSE ITEMS ASKED FOR IN THE GRAY BOX, AT THE BOTTOM OF THE PAGE
20 POINTS/ COMPLETED ASSIGNMENT OBTAINING SOME OF THE OBJECTIVES IN THE GREEN BOX	20 POINTS/ COMPLETED ASSIGNMENT SHOWING AN ATTEMPT TO USE CONCEPT SHOWN IN ART WORK	20 POINTS/ COMPLETED ASSIGNMENT SHOWING AN ATTEMPT TO USE MATERIALS OR TECHNIQUES	20 POINTS/ COMPLETED PROJECT SHOWING AN UNDERSTANDING OF THE UNIT BUT DID NOT ACCOMPLISH SOME ITEMS ASKED FOR IN THE GRAY BOX, AT THE BOTTOM OF THE PAGE
15 POINTS/ COMPLETED ASSIGNMENT BUT DID NOT OBTAIN OBJECTIVES IN THE GREEN BOX	15 POINTS/ COMPLETED ASSIGNMENT DID NOT USE CONCEPT SHOWN IN ART WORK	15 POINTS/ COMPLETED ASSIGNMENT DID NOT USE MATERIALS CORRECTLY OR TRY THE TECHNIQUES SHOWN	15 POINTS/ COMPLETED PROJECT DID NOT SHOW UNDERSTANDING OF THE UNIT OR ITEMS ASKED FOR IN THE GRAY BOX, AT THE BOTTOM OF THE PAGE

Note: If you do not see how the student accomplished the objectives asked for, do ask them about it. Sometimes they understood very well and will be able to tell you how they accomplished the task in the drawing. This is valid. Remember that getting a visual idea across clearly is a process that takes time. Allow the student to grow into it.

Bibliography

Bennett, William J., *The Book of Virtues, A Treasury of Great Moral Stories.* Simon and Schuster, New York, 1993.

Gombrich, E.H., *The Story of Art.* Phaidon Press Inc., New York, NY, pocket edition 2006.

Jacobus, Lee A., *The Bedford Introduction to Drama*, Bedford/St. Martin's, Boston, New York, Fifth Edition 2005.

Janson, H.W. *History of Art, A Survey of the Major Visual Arts from the Dawn of History to the Present Day.* Prentice-Hall, Inc. Englewood Cliffs, N.J. and Harry N. Abrams, Inc., New York, 1974

Lee, Sherman E., *A History of Far Eastern Art*. Prentice-Hall, Inc. and Harry N. Abrams, Inc., New York, 1973.

Let me suggest some excellent reading material for newcomers to art who want a better understanding of world art:

The Story of Art by E.H. Gombrich
Published by Phaidon Press Inc.

This book is a great introduction to the entire story of art from cave painting to the later part of the 20th century. Its short chapters and conversational manner make it easy to understand. The writing is simple. Gombrich does not use excessive wordiness. Here students and parents will get a concise, clearly organized narrative. Gombrich has incredible insight into human nature and makes connections so that we see art as a continual flow. Each artist takes part in the tradition of his time and Gombrich clearly points out what those traditions and mindsets were. Artwork also hints toward future developments as one work inspires new ideas for other artists. These connections give better understanding to human thought and Gombrich is not afraid to discuss the rich spiritual heritage that took hold in Europe from the medieval period through the Renaissance. Those art enthusiasts who would rather look than read will be pleased to know that over half of the book is devoted to pictures. This book should be a first choice for all newcomers to art.

Sell your books at
World of Books!
Go to sell.worldofbooks.com
and get an instant price

ART / EDUCATION

Artistic Pursuits Second Edition offers students the opportunity to discover their own creative strengths in the arts. The elements of art and composition are explored through beautiful color reproductions of World Art.

- Text written in conversational manner means student can work independently
- Full year course in one book
- Two lessons per week
- Four unique projects in each unit include creative exercise, art history and appreciation, techniques, and exploration of various subject matter

"(My daughter) has been tackling the book solo. She raves about the presentation, and has already begun to improve...In addition; I see her enjoying art more."

Homeschool Parent – Heather Schwarzen / Washington

"This curriculum works. It makes artists! My children are really learning to draw, not just copy someone else's artwork, and to use their drawing in their daily lives. And it is so easy to use."

Homeschool Parent – Nancy Gorman/ Massachusetts

"...at times you discover an art or drawing program that is so easy-to-use, open-ended, and brimming with all sorts of exciting possibilities that your fingers just itch for a pencil and paper, and time to play around. And this was certainly the case with Artistic Pursuits. It keeps the subject on a level as understandable for a beginner as it is for someone with some artistic experience."

Homeschooler – Jessica Schneider / Illinois

**Published by
Artistic Pursuits Inc.
www.artisticpursuits.com**

Non-consumable
Use this book again and again!

Junior High Book One, USA $42.95

ISBN 978-0-9815982-6-0

This book has shown thousands of students how to create original works of art while laying a solid educational foundation under their feet. Your role as parent/teacher is to praise the results and encourage. Isn't that what you want to do anyway? Start today!